For mothers everywhere

Beatnik

Beatnik Publishing
PO Box 8276, Symonds Street, Auckland 1150, New Zealand.

First published in 2016 by Beatnik Publishing.
Reprinted in 2018 by Beantik Publishing.
Revised and published in 2021 by Beatnik Publishing.

Foreword: Anne Stephenson

Art Director & Illustrator: Sally Greer
Typeface: Ashbury
Type Designer: Dieter Hofrichter

Printed and bound in China.

FSC www.fsc.org MIX Paper from responsible sources FSC™ C007683

ISBN 978-0-9922648-4-0 - Original
ISBN 978-0-9951423-2-9 - Revised Edition

golden month

Caring for the World's Mothers After Childbirth

Jenny Allison

Contents

Foreword

Thank you, Jenny, for asking me to write the foreword to your book, *Golden Month*. It is a pleasure and also a responsibility for the subject of this book, the care of mothers after childbirth, is of considerable importance. For 36 years I have been working as a general practitioner, 26 years of these in an inner-city London community. The care of new mothers has been a large part of my work, as it is for most general practitioners. I am constantly in touch with the rich diversity that this city has to offer, for example over 300 languages are spoken in London schools, and I have been party to a wide variety of experiences of new mothers, some supported by their families and communities and others very much alone. From my experience I know how essential good care is in those first few weeks and how it is the key to a fulfilling motherhood, personhood, family and community life. I can think of a teenage mother who lives with her extended family. Her baby is the families' baby and she has their full support and experience to draw on. Another new mother has recently come to London from another country and her husband, whose family lives outside London, has been her only support. He is very kind but works long hours and she has felt very lonely and isolated and has only slowly, with help, built up a network of her own. A mother in an arranged marriage suffered abuse and a psychotic breakdown. Fortunately with the support of her family and mental health services she has made a full recovery and her little boy is a delight. I am also a mother and I became very aware of how much new mothers need after giving birth myself. I remember that wonderful morning when my daughter was born and how open and vulnerable I felt.For a number of weeks the thought of venturing out onto London streets or even watching an action movie was too much. I am conscious of the fast pace of life in London, the mobility of the population (London has some boroughs where population mobility is greater than 35% per annum), the breakdown of the extended family, and the financial pressures. This is true of many places in the world these days. Most new mothers, unless they are part of a very established community that is supporting them, get very little time for rest or opportunities for being cared for. When I look at the resources on new motherhood available to the health professionals in the UK (for example the National Institute for Health and Care Excellence Guidelines on Postnatal Care, CG37, December 2014), I realise that they are very much focussed on structures, plans and what can go wrong. The UK Department of Health book, *Birth to Five* that is available to all new mothers, puts the responsibility firmly onto the mother: 'If you don't take care of yourself you will end up run down and exhausted and you will not have the energy you need to make a good job of being a parent'. I can understand where those who wrote both these documents are coming from. There is a certain reality in what they say. However let's do all we can to take the responsibility off a new mother in those first weeks and make it an easy, nourishing, and happy time for her and her baby. The cultural practices of Africa, Asia, the Pacific, Europe, South America and New Zealand that Jenny describes have much to teach us in this regard. We have many examples in our global communities to learn from. Rest, nourishment, support and positive regard for a new mother builds a strong foundation and prevents a thousand ills. I consider that the health of a society is not measured by its economic development. It is reflected in the way it treats its mothers and fathers. Since reading this book I am certainly more determined to do all I can to make this happen for those new mothers I work with. It will make all the difference. Finally I ask you to read Jenny's book carefully and thoughtfully. The message is profound. Thank you, Jenny, for writing this book.

Anne Stephenson
February 2015

Acknowledgements

This book is the result of a team effort: it could not have come into being without the women who generously told me their stories and insights, those who offered their valuable information on the postpartum in medicine and anthropology, and those who gave their support from the very beginning of the project.

First of all, I want to thank those who contributed directly to the book: Ngangouma, Hawa, Kadjiatou, Puja, Lucia, Galuafi, Carolina, Anjalika, Huria, Tineke, Phoebe, Daliya and Josefa for their stories, and Anne for her beautiful foreword, written from the heart.

Many thanks to naturopaths Sheran Marra, Loula George and anthropologist Dr Jane Horan who shared their valuable knowledge, to midwives Carly Francis, Dawn Holland and Jennifer Fletcher who shared theirs, and to Rona Wang, Dr Tinh Thong Nguyen, Dr Priya Punjabi, Professor Tian Cong Huo, and Wai Mason for their insights into traditional medical practices.

For their wonderful encouragement, support and practical help, many thanks, firstly, to my husband Boubacar, my daughter Frances, son Yacouba and my sisters Judy and Fran; and for all the different ways the following people have helped: Helen Palmer, Robin Allison, Leslie Brokenshire, Judith Ackroyd, Karen Stacey, Suzanne Downie, Christopher Sarson, Inda Yansané, Val Wisely, Aisha Shawish, Dr Fe Day, Lotte Wotherspoon, Marg Leniston, Dr Sue Cochrane, Paddy McBride, Orlando Garcia, Di and Will Maudlin, Pia McKay, Vardi Benesh-Raviv and Juleen Tjauw.

Finally, my very special thanks go to Sally Greer, Karen McKenzie, Kitki Tong, Alena Kavka and Kyle Ranudo of Beatnik Publishing and publishing editor Briar Towers.

Introduction

The postpartum is a unique period of transition in a woman's life. In just a few weeks, as she recovers her strength and learns to mother her new baby, a woman's body and mind undergo changes of unparalleled intensity. She enters a rite of passage which literally changes who she is, and learns many things about life and herself in the process. She also begins a relationship with her newborn which will be a template for the baby's trusting relationships with other human beings, in a bond which will last their lifetimes.

Care of mothers after childbirth, the subject of this book, is an issue of universal social importance. Good care in the six-week postpartum period is crucial to the mother's health and well-being, and can have lasting benefits, not only to her health and relationship with her newborn baby, but more widely, to her family and community as well.

In the following chapters I explore the changes that take place in women's bodies and minds during this six-week period, and the specific needs that arise from them. I discuss the general principles of good postpartum care, and the ways we can apply these principles in our modern lifestyles. We will encounter different cultural practices and hear mothers' postpartum stories from around the world. For some women this book will offer a validation of their own traditions for keeping healthy and making a good recovery after childbirth; for other women who do not have strong traditions to follow, it will offer practical guidance. For all women, I hope that the ideas and practices described below will resonate with their own feelings about what they need and how they expect to be looked after during their 'Golden Month'.

The 'Golden Month' is one of the names the Chinese use for the four to six weeks after childbirth: it reflects the expectation in Chinese culture that this will be an enriching and happy moment for the new mother. Traditionally the Golden Month is a period of celebration for everyone in the family when the mother rests and is given special care, food and advice for six weeks, or longer, until she feels fully recovered. She is the focus of attention in the family, and is acknowledged and praised for her gift of a child to the family. She also works on improving her own health: it is believed this time is a watershed in terms of women's health, and that caring well for the mother not only ensures her good health for the future, but can even resolve past health issues.

Throughout the world there are similar strong traditions and rituals of postnatal care which are still being practiced today. They are given a variety of names. In Latin American countries, the six weeks is called the *cuarentena*, or *resguardo* (which means 'protection'), in India, Russia, Romania, Greece and many African and Arab countries, it is 'the 40 days' (in the various languages of these countries). In China, women talk about *zuo yue zi* or 'doing the month' as they follow the traditions of the Golden Month. Below is a scene I witnessed in Mali, West Africa. It speaks for the many mothers who are fortunate to have such favourable conditions in their postpartum, and who can enjoy the benefits this care brings:

A group of three women sit talking under the shade of a mango tree. It is mid-morning in a courtyard in Bamako, Mali, and this relatively cool spot is the centre of family social life. The women sit under one side of the huge tree, while on the other side the cooking fire for the family lunch is being fanned. Wood smoke and the smell of frying tomatoes drift towards us. The sounds of children and chickens are amplified by the red mud walls of the compound. The women are discussing childbirth and the ways that they are looked after in the weeks following the births of their babies. They talk about their '40 days' of rest. 'The 40 days' is an institution for Malian women.

The group consists of a businesswoman and mother of five, a retired farmer and mother of ten, and a new mother, Kadjiatou, with her second baby, Seydou, on her lap. They talk with pride about their tradition, and about how most women, even in the city and those working in government, do 'the 40 days'. Seydou is two months old and Kadjiatou has just finished two months of being cared for by her sister-in-law. She is looking contented. At one point she indicates the mango tree above her. 'I feel so good in myself and so healthy that I could just run and climb that tree,' she says.

Kadjiatou didn't have adequate support after her first birth, her daughter. She was living in an isolated area of the Sahel where her husband was posted as a paramedic, and she had not been able to do her '40 days' because there were no relatives or community network there to look after her. She said it had been very hard. By contrast she was well looked after this time around, and both she and her baby looked strong.

These women (whom we will meet again in Chapter Five) see good postpartum care of the mother as a right, not a privilege. Even in a country such as Mali which is economically poor, all women working in formal employment are given two and a half months' paid maternity leave to do their '40 days' and recover after childbirth. Doing 'the 40 days' in both the countryside and the city is fully supported by the men and women of the family and by the community.

Care of the mother has become a neglected aspect of postnatal care in Western society. In the past, before it became the norm in the early twentieth century for women to be hospitalized for childbirth, the birth and the 'lying-in' period after birth were attended by the midwife, friends and relatives, who gave practical and emotional support to the mother. This activity has been described as 'social childbirth' since it was a community event for women. It allowed the mother to rest for several weeks, or more, while she regained her strength, established breastfeeding and got to know her baby.[1]

In current Western medical practice, however, while the newborn is a focus of attention, it is not the same for the mother. The postpartum has been called the 'Cinderella period' by midwives who are concerned at the current lack of awareness of its importance.[2] We no longer talk about it as the 'lying-in' period, or by any popular name, for that matter; it is known only by its medical term, the postpartum. While great emphasis is placed on the birth and the baby's welfare, there is less focus on the mother's well-being after birth. Statistics for postnatal women's health in many Western countries show rates of postnatal depression at over 20% according to some estimates.[3,4] Researchers have shown that good postpartum support can have a protective effect against developing postpartum depression, and that the converse is also true, that neglect of the mother's needs after giving birth is a contributing factor to depression.[5]

Simply resting after childbirth is no longer given the importance that it had only a generation or two ago. We live in a modern society which operates on pressured time schedules and it is not easy to find space in this environment where we can quietly restore our health and energy. We have been taught that women can do anything. This is wonderful, but it doesn't mean that we can do everything. We are also taught that independence is a virtue, without recognizing that interdependence is also a virtue and is important at times like giving birth. With such external and internal pressures to perform well, in addition to trying to survive financially, there is the risk that we forget to listen to our needs and intuitions around the biological rhythms of birth and breastfeeding. This often means we are now expected, and expect of ourselves, to continue on with our lives as soon as possible after we have given birth.

There are other contributing factors also which prevent women from taking the rest they need. In recent years the older women of the family have become less available to care for the new mother. Economic pressure may mean they live in other cities or are still out in the workforce, as are our sisters and friends. In immigrant communities there may also be a lack of understanding of postnatal rituals by healthcare professionals. The result is a lack of support and care. Yet simple preventive measures can greatly improve the health and well-being of mothers, and this is understood by many grandmothers who want to be available to care for their daughters and daughters-in-law. In Asian immigrant communities, for example, caring for the new mother is still given priority by grandmothers and aunts, some of whom may come great distances from their home countries to look after the new mother and baby.

The insights of the Chinese medical tradition feature prominently in this book. One of the strengths of Chinese medicine lies in its emphasis on maintaining good health and preventing disease, which makes it highly relevant to the care of the mother after childbirth. It is also my own specialty. The main reason, however, is that it is a good example of a medical tradition based on the human body as an energy system. Chinese medicine explains thoroughly and well, in its own terms, the reasoning behind the postnatal practices shared by so many traditions around the world. When the postpartum is viewed from an energetic, as well as a modern biomedical and social perspective, a holistic viewpoint can be achieved which greatly broadens our understanding of the processes involved in a woman's postpartum recovery and transition to motherhood.

In my clinical practice, I have noticed that there is a pattern of mothers coming for help some months or even years after they have given birth. They report they are exhausted, have a depressed mood, keep getting colds or flu, are finding it hard to lose excess weight or are suffering from chronic backache and other pains. Sometimes they have difficulty getting pregnant again because they have not recovered their strength after the previous birth. These women often comment that they did not have enough rest and support after giving birth, in spite of doing what they thought was normal to look after themselves. Their symptoms were, to a large degree, I believe, a consequence of this.

Even though it is a necessity, and, as I shall show, the best thing for mothers' health to have several weeks of care and support after childbirth, most mothers in Western countries do not get this essential rest for six weeks that is a part of many traditions worldwide.

In the Māori tradition of New Zealand a new mother's status is sacred. The mother is called *te whare tangata*, the house of humanity. She is referred to as 'the canoe that conveys one generation to the next', and motherhood in general carries a high status. Birth reinforces her sacredness. Therefore one of the most important times to honour motherhood and the mother is after she has given birth. Traditional Māori , Malian and many other cultures recognize the mother's special status and needs after childbirth: Kadjiatou's experience with her second child is normal throughout West Africa. Her mother-in-law, grandmother Ngangouma, concluded the meeting under the tree with this advice to me:

> Please tell your women they should rest for 40 days (after birth), stop work and look after

> themselves. It doesn't matter when you return to work, there will always be money to be made. When you recover you can start back at work again. If you tell them and they listen to you, that would be great...

A key message of this book is for women to listen to their own needs – emotional and physical – after birth. It is not easy to do this in a society with time and performance pressures. It is also not easy when the unhealthy 'drive yourself to perfection' mentality of our ubiquitous celebrity culture pulls women in an opposing direction, encouraging them back to the gym in search of pre-pregnant body shapes with the idea that they should quickly get back to normal in all areas of life. Many of the mothers who shared their stories in the course of this project have provided a welcome counterpoint to this attitude. They promote a set of values which allows women to tune in to their own being and normalize at their own pace after giving birth.

The book is arranged in six chapters.

Chapter One is an overview of the physiological changes that occur after childbirth. Two perspectives are used, the modern biomedical, or Western medical, view and the traditional Chinese medical view. The two different views complement each other in informing the reader of the medical facts of the postpartum, and of its unique importance.

Chapter Two discusses the benefits of good care of the mother and the impact this has on her well-being, the baby and the rest of the family.

The main guidelines for good care are presented in Chapters Three and Four. These chapters are the foundation of the practice promoted by the book. The four most important components of good care are rest, warmth and/or massage, diet, and support. These were the common factors of good care amongst the different cultures whose women I interviewed.

Chapter Five consists of the postnatal stories of women from around the world. In it they discuss their own experiences and the traditions they come from.

The final chapter discusses the challenges in improving care of new mothers, including change at the level of family and the community.

***

1. R. W. Wertz and D. C. Wertz. *Lying-In: A History of Childbirth in America* (Yale University Press, 1989), p.4.

2. S. Wickham (ed.). *Midwifery: Best Practice vol.5* (Butterworth Heinemann Elsevier, 2008)

3. S. Byrom, G. Edwards and D. Bick (eds). *Essential Midwifery Practice: Postnatal Care* (Wiley Blackwell, 2010).

4. L. J. Miller and E. M. LaRusso. 'Preventing Postpartum Depression', *Psychiatric Clinics of North America,* March 2011; 34(1): p.53.

5. R. W. Wertz and D. C. Wertz. *Lying-In: A History of Childbirth in America* (Yale University Press, 1989), p.256.

Chapter One

The Postnatal Period – Modern Biomedicine and Chinese Medicine Perspectives

In this chapter I will explain the physiology of the postpartum period from two perspectives, the modern biomedical system, and the Chinese medical system which is based on the idea of energy flow in the body. I encourage you to explore the medical details of what happens after childbirth as there are very good medical as well as social reasons for looking after new mothers in the Golden Month.

Modern medicine

The postpartum has only recently become a focus of attention and research in modern healthcare, with the recognition that it is an important period of change and adjustment for parents.[1] In modern medicine the six-week period after the birth is called the *postpartum* or the *postnatal* period. These two terms are used interchangeably throughout the book. It is a time of major bodily and psychological change after the birth of the baby, during which the mother recovers from the exertion of the labour, or in the case of a birth by caesarean section, from surgery, and also undergoes many social adjustments. It is sometimes referred to as the 'fourth trimester', implying that the process which began at conception is still to be completed in this final six-week to three-month phase. It is beginning to be acknowledged once more in Western society as an important phase whose culmination is the woman's return into society as a mother.

Looking first at the physical changes, in this phase the woman reverts back to the non-pregnant hormonal state. Once the placenta is delivered after the birth of her baby, the hormones progesterone and oestrogen (high levels of which are contained in placenta) drop quickly to non-pregnant levels over a week, while other pregnancy hormones such as human chorionic gonadotropin (HCG) can take up to ten days. These changes are associated with changes in the neurotransmitters serotonin and dopamine, which affect feelings of well-being. Between 50% and 80% of mothers experience mood swings at this time, commonly described as the 'baby blues'. One reason is that levels of the mood enhancer serotonin drop, or the brain's ability to uptake serotonin is decreased after birth, and it can even take a year or more to return to normal, especially if the mother is in a stressful situation or exhausted from poor health or overwork.[2] While dopamine and endorphins (which are also mood enhancers) can remain high for some weeks after the birth, the effects of lowered serotonin, with an accompanying lowering of mood and increase in anxiety, often begin to be felt several weeks afterward, as dopamine and endorphin levels slowly drop after the birth and its intensity.

At the same time, prolactin and cortisol initiate milk production. Cortisol is an especially interesting hormone from the perspective of the postnatal period. Cortisol is produced in the adrenal glands as part of the 'fight or flight' mechanism and has wide-ranging effects on the body and mind. It is a useful response to danger when the body needs to be galvanized into action. If it remains high after the birth because of stress, fear or overexertion while the body is still weak, it is as if the body still perceives danger to its survival and keeps overproducing 'fight or flight' cortisol. High cortisol is associated with blood clotting, memory loss, weight gain, poor immunity and an increased risk of depression. At the extreme, if cortisol is overproduced over a long period, the adrenal glands become exhausted and can no longer produce cortisol properly. At this point the mother feels very exhausted and 'low', especially in the morning, and her milk production suffers. The health of her adrenals therefore plays a big part in her health and well-being.

The release of the milk itself is the responsibility of the hormone oxytocin, which also produces the contractions that help to stop bleeding after delivery and contract the uterus down to its normal pre-pregnant position. Oxytocin is a neuromodulating hormone which produces feelings of calm, trust, connection and generosity. It can dramatically enhance feelings of well-being and help in coping with the changes that are taking place at this time. It also enhances the efficiency of the mother's digestion and helps her to absorb nutrients well. According to an oxytocin expert, Kerstin Uvnas-Moberg, it produces a calming antidote to stress with long-term positive health benefits.[3] Oxytocin is stimulated during birth and by holding, touching and breastfeeding the baby. It is inhibited by fear and anxiety. In fact, as all of these hormones, serotonin, dopamine, cortisol and oxytocin, are disrupted by stress it becomes clear how important it is to keep a pleasant, calm 'nesting place' for the new mother to rest in.

Aside from changes at the hormonal or chemical level, there are also major bodily changes as the uterus, cervix, vagina and perineum heal themselves. Some of this can take six to seven weeks, such as the placental site in the uterus. The bleeding that happens after giving birth (called 'lochia') continues, getting gradually lighter and lighter, until the uterus has healed at around six weeks. When it stops it is the sign in most cultures that the postpartum is over. While the cervix, which is bruised and swollen after delivery, normally heals after 48 hours, the vagina and perineum may take weeks to heal. The vagina is more vascular during pregnancy due to increased progesterone and may stay swollen for several weeks, while the vaginal mucosa (the cells lining the vagina) can take six to ten weeks to heal. If there are grazes, tears or an episiotomy (cut) was made in the perineum, it can take many weeks to heal, whether or not there were stitches inserted to help repair the wound, and there may even be pain and difficulty moving for months. This is the healing process after a vaginal delivery; there may be additional emotional trauma if there were complications during the birth or even if it was very quick. If the baby was born through a c-section, the wound in the lower abdomen from the surgery must heal, as well as the usual lochia and any additional trauma to the body and mind. The uterus also returns to its normal position in the pelvis more slowly than after a vaginal delivery.

Structurally, the body is changed after birth: whatever the means of delivery, the ligaments around the joints are still soft after the birth due to the influence of progesterone during pregnancy and the joints take time to stabilize. Finally, fluid balance, and blood volume and flow, which depend on the heart and kidneys, need up to six weeks to normalize after birth. The heart, for example, can take several weeks to reach its pre-pregnancy output, a process which may be hampered if there has been a lot of blood loss. During pregnancy the amount of pressure that is needed to maintain the blood flow to the placenta means the flow of blood is faster and the heart is pumping more blood with each beat. After she gives birth, the mother maintains only her own circulation. Her output is now lower. Most women will lose about 500ml of blood when they give birth, which means a lower blood volume. The result is a slowing down of the blood flow in the deep veins, which can make women vulnerable to circulatory problems such as clotting. This is particularly true if the woman has given birth to twins, or is an older mother.[4] Clotting is also a risk influenced by stress – the more adrenaline produced, the higher the cortisol level, which in turn means a higher clotting factor.

I will now turn to the Chinese medicine perspective for its ideas on the postnatal period and examine how this tradition supports and cares for the new mother.

Chinese medicine

The first Chinese medical textbook was produced over 2000 years ago (*c.* 500 BC) with a text entitled *Huang Di Nei Jing*, or 'The Yellow Emperor's Classic of Internal Medicine'. Ever since then Chinese medicine has undergone a continuous process of developing and refining its theory and clinical practice, and over time it has established many different schools of thought and traditions. Chinese medicine spread early on in its history to Japan, Korea and Vietnam, producing a variety of styles of practice, here discussed under the umbrella name of Oriental medicine, or traditional East Asian medicine. In the last century, Oriental medicine has received some acceptance and integration into mainstream Western systems as an effective healing method for many situations and conditions. Like all energy-based healing systems, the Chinese approach to the human body and mind is so different from that of modern biomedicine that talking about it can be like speaking another language.

For this reason a few of the key ideas need to be introduced for those who are not familiar with its view of the body as an interconnected energy system.

Underlying all theory in Chinese medicine is the awareness that human beings are connected to the natural world and the universe around us. Health depends on living harmoniously in our world. At a simple level this means dressing, eating and behaving in accordance with the seasons, the weather, and the natural patterns of day and night. At the foundation of all existence are the concepts of *yin* and *yang*. These are two opposing but interdependent forces which exist in dynamic balance with one another. Yin is associated with winter and with an image of the dark side of a mountain. It is moistening, cooling and nourishing. Yang is associated with summer, and with the sunny or bright side of the mountain. Yang is warmth, activity and transformation. In nature, yin gives way to yang as winter changes to summer, and vice versa.

The other idea which is fundamental to Chinese medicine is that human beings are mirrors of the universe. What goes on in the macrocosm of the natural world is mirrored in the activities of the human body. Chinese medicine uses images which come from nature to describe both normal and disordered processes in the human body, so we describe yin and yang also within the body, and the organs and their functions belong to the different elements found in nature, such as fire, water, earth, etc.

Just as all things in the universe are interconnected, our bodily systems (organ functions, nervous and immune systems, etc.) are also interconnected. The foundation of health is seen as the dynamic balance of yin with yang, and of the organ systems with one another. They interact so closely that if one function goes out of balance every other part of the body will be affected. Thus Chinese medicine maintains an integrated, or holistic, view of the human body, wherein it is important to pay attention to the whole body and mind as one. In a very simple example, if someone becomes too yang, they will tend to overheat and the yin or cooling aspect of the body will eventually be depleted. At this stage the balance of yin and yang is disturbed and the foundation of one's health is affected. After childbirth, the balance of yin and yang becomes unstable, because a woman has used so much of her yang energy through the transformative process of birth. Therefore she tends to feel cold easily. In caring for her after birth, the yang must be supported as she returns to balance.

In Chinese medicine, good health is described as the ability to adapt to a changing environment, thus maintaining a balance of yin and yang is essential to being healthy. These ideas show that the Chinese medical tradition places a lot of emphasis on disease prevention and maintaining or improving well-being, and for this reason postnatal care of the mother has always been an important part of maintaining women's health.

There are three other concepts which are relevant to our subject. They are *jing*, *qi* and *shen* and are often grouped together under the title of the 'Three Treasures of Health'. All three are expressions of energy in the body, and each one depends upon the other to remain healthy.

Jing

Jing is translated as 'essence'. It is considered to be the deepest source of our energy, which runs through the generations from our parents and those before them, and it is therefore very precious. Essence or jing is stored in the lower abdomen and relates to the kidneys, adrenal glands and reproductive organs. It is the basis of all yin (nourishment) and yang (activity) in the body. It is important for libido and fertility in both sexes. A man's essence is concentrated in his sperm as 'white gold', while a woman's essence is expressed in the quality of her eggs and in her ability to conceive and remain pregnant. An embryo is the gathering of the jing of both parents into a concentrated form. If the jing is not strong, there may be difficulties in conception, and a baby from parents with weak jing may have delicate health.

Jing is made up of a 'pre-heaven' and a 'post-heaven' aspect: together these form the basis of our constitution. There are rough parallels here with genetics (pre-heaven jing) and epigenetics, the mechanism by which changes in the environment can alter our genes (a part of post-heaven jing). The epigenetic aspect is at the root of the belief that the months spent in the mother's womb are worth many years out in the world, in terms of future health. This is supported by modern biomedical research which has shown that the mother's diet can influence genetic expression in the foetus and the tendency to certain diseases in adulthood. But post-heaven jing is more than this: when energy is produced by breathing and eating, some is used in daily life and some, the energy that is left over from this process, is stored each night as post-heaven jing. Thus breathing and eating well are ways of preserving the constitution we are born with. Jing is also the matrix for the formation of blood. It combines with the pure substances derived from food to help in the creation of blood, and in this way it is the basis of our physical, constitutional strength.

From a practical standpoint, jing is like savings in the bank and therefore it is most important to conserve. In general, the more jing you have, the more likely it is you will live a long and healthy life. Apart from eating and breathing correctly, ways of conserving jing include pacing oneself through life rather than rushing, and not pushing ourselves beyond what our body is telling us we can do. A classic way to rebuild lost jing is to rest without thoughts, an idea that is refined in practices such as meditation or quiet mindfulness. Resting in this way allows the mind to disengage, which in turn calms the emotions and settles the body, providing the conditions for restoration.

Carrying a baby and giving birth draws greatly on our jing, and after giving birth there needs to be a period of time when it can be restored and built up again. If this happens as it should, the new mother can return to the normal routines of her life feeling replenished. But if she has too many births too close together or not enough chance to recover in the first crucial weeks after the birth, then her jing can become seriously depleted. It is hard to regain at this stage, even if she rests a lot later on.

When I was studying Chinese medicine I used to wonder how women in some cultures, mostly rural societies with a heavy physical workload, managed to have many children and not exhaust their jing. But when I started talking to these women, I realized how careful they were to look after themselves after childbirth. They told me that with each successive birth the mother received the same level of care, and sometimes for many months if there were complications at the birth. In this way women could go on to have more children and remain strong and healthy.

The myth still exists about 'tribal' women stopping behind a bush to deliver their baby and then going back to work in the field, but in speaking with these women it was clearly not the case. Even if they gave birth easily, they rested for at least six weeks afterwards, according to their traditions. When the system broke down it was usually because the woman was not near her usual caregivers, or if there was extreme poverty and the breakdown of her community around her.

Qi

Qi is a difficult term to translate exactly, and I will use its name in Chinese for that reason. It could generally be thought of as 'vital force', but it means more than this. Qi permeates all things in the universe and connects us with all life. It is what makes life and the universe happen. At birth, qi condenses, and at death, it disperses: nothing is gained or lost in this process. It can be described as the building block of the universe.

Qi creates warmth, movement and flow in our bodies. When it flows well we have a sense of well-being. When qi is not flowing well there are two reasons. There is either plenty of qi but it is 'constrained' (often from emotional stress), or else it cannot move adequately because there is not enough of it. When qi does not flow well there may be a combination of both qi deficiency and qi constraint at the same time.

After birth we need to pay attention to both scenarios. However it is the second scenario, that there is not enough qi to move well, that needs special attention. The act of giving birth uses a lot of qi, and if the woman is rested and relaxed the labour is likely to progress smoothly, since the qi is plentiful and is flowing well. After birth the situation is different. The new mother's qi is relatively depleted by the effort of labour, no matter how young and strong she is. After birth, therefore, is the time to care for oneself by receiving and benefitting from the qi of others, whether it is in receiving the reassuring care of an elder, consuming a nicely served hot meal from a friend, or enjoying a massage (which has the added benefit of someone else's hands moving qi as well as giving qi).

The warming, dynamic aspect of qi is called the *yang qi*. As a lot of yang qi has been consumed in pushing out the baby, the mother's yang qi is also depleted after childbirth and she is vulnerable to cold. To avoid cold 'invading' the body, including the joints and digestive system, she needs to avoid cold water and cold food, and being exposed to cold wind and draughts.

Qi is also necessary to build 'blood'. (The concept of 'blood' in Chinese medicine is wider than in Western medicine). Qi produces blood, and blood circulates with qi throughout the vessels of the body. At the same time blood nourishes the organs which create qi. Thus they depend upon one another. When blood is lost during childbirth, qi is also lost. Childbirth is therefore especially depleting, since qi is lost through both exertion and loss of blood. In Chinese medicine, the stomach and digestion must be strong to produce good qi and blood. Therefore it is extremely important in this situation to support the function of the stomach so that it can effectively transform food into usable qi. This is the reason that so much emphasis is placed on diet for the new mother in Chinese medicine: the postnatal diet consists of foods which specifically strengthen qi and blood, but also support the digestion. This is discussed in more detail in Chapter Three.

Blood is the foundation of breast milk and, as a living substance derived from blood, breast milk also carries qi with it. This makes it particularly nourishing for the baby. The qi both vitalizes the milk and ensures that it flows smoothly so that the let-down reflex can deliver the milk into the milk ducts. Once again, qi must be sufficient in quantity and flowing well for the breasts to function properly in their new role. Qi may be strong enough to produce sufficient blood and therefore milk, but if it can't move freely lactation will be poor. If the qi is constrained there is also a danger of mastitis: two circulatory pathways, or meridians, pass across the breast, the pathways of the stomach and liver. The qi, carried with the blood along these pathways, may be constrained by eating food which is too rich and indigestible and/or by emotional constraint from unexpressed emotions or excess anger.

Shen

Modern Chinese medical textbooks translate *shen* as 'spirit', 'intelligence' or 'consciousness'. Shen is the most refined energy of the Three Treasures. It guides and rules the qi within us and gives us the capacity to know wisdom. Shen, or spirit, manifests as the shine in our eyes, and when it is strong the prognosis for recovery from disease is good.

In Vietnam it is said that the mother is the most beautiful she will ever be after the birth of her first child. There is a cleansing effect from the qi and blood moving strongly through her, and there is also a strengthening of her spirit from the spiritual connection and growth that is possible with the process of becoming a mother. In giving birth we have the privilege of connecting with the source of life, and the power of this makes us beautiful. At the same time our shen is also vulnerable and easily disturbed. Ngangouma Traore, the Malian grandmother whom we will meet again later, says that after birth 'the tomb is open'. In Brazil, post-partum women are said to be 'open'.[5] The term for the 40-day rest period in Portuguese is actually *resguardo* from the word *resguardar*, to protect.

Spirit or shen is housed in the Heart. This Heart (with a capital H) is not just the physical organ of the heart, which happens to be the most energetically powerful organ in the body in itself, but it is also an energy system. The Heart includes the heart organ, but is more than that. The Heart gives the capacity for love and joy, and it is where the emotions are kept in balance. In Chinese medicine, the Heart is called the 'supreme ruler' of all systems in the body and mind and it belongs to the element of fire. On the one hand, a strong shen nourishes the body: when the shen is calm and there is love, the fire of Heart is able to descend to warm and replenish jing. On the other hand, a strong body nourishes shen: when the blood of the Heart is full, the shen is strong and can remain calm. When qi, blood and jing are weakened after childbirth, the shen needs special care to help it remain stable.

Giving birth and falling in love with the new baby gives the possibility for a unique opening of the Heart, which nourishes the mother's shen, that of the baby and of all those close to the mother. A quiet, calm environment is necessary for this to happen.

***

1. S. Pairman, S. Tracy, C. Thorogood and C. Pincombe et al. *Midwifery: Preparation for Practice*. 2nd edn (Churchill Livingston, 2010), p.576.

2. F. Naish and J. Roberts. *The Natural Way to Better Birth and Bonding* (Doubleday, 2009), p.226.

3. S. Buckley. *Gentle Birth, Gentle Mothering* (Celestial Arts, 2009), p.103.

4. L. Fiengo, F. Bucci, G. Patrizi, et al. 'Postpartum Deep Vein Thrombosis and Pulmonary Embolism in Twin Pregnancy', *Thrombosis Journal,* 2013; 11(4), http://www.thrombosisjournal.com/content/11/1/4. See also, https://www.clinicalkey.com/topics/surgery/deep-vein-thrombosis.html.

5. B. Piperata. 'Forty Days and Forty Nights: A Biocultural Perspective on Postpartum Practices in the Amazon', *Social Science and Medicine,* 2008; 67(7).

Chapter Two

The Benefits of Good Care of the Mother - Well-being, Bonding, Laying Foundations of Future Health

The greatest benefit of caring well for the mother after childbirth is that she will have a sense of well-being, strength and pride in herself. This may seem obvious but its importance does need to be underlined. If the mother feels well, her recovery will be easier, she will bond better with her baby, establish a good milk supply, and feel more able to make the adjustments to her role as a mother that the new baby's arrival brings.

Mothers play a central role in the well-being of the family and community around them. As the *Ashtanga Sangraha*, an ancient Ayurvedic (traditional Indian) medical text, says:

> The woman plays the key role in this *ashrama* (i.e. family life). Hence the health of the woman should be protected by all means. If woman is protected, in turn she will protect the whole community. - *Acharya Vagbhata, c. 400 AD*

This remains as true now as when it was written over 1500 years ago. As well as benefitting herself, a well cared for mother benefits her partner and her whole family. The arrival of a new baby means a period of adjustment for everyone in the family and extended family, and this is made much easier if the mother is well. Investing time and effort in her recovery benefits the family dynamic in the long term and helps to create a healthy family culture of respect and regard for motherhood.

Since the pace of modern life has become increasingly fast and traditions of care of the mother in the period after birth have declined, women may face the postpartum period with feelings of worry or fear. This phase of motherhood may be both wonderful and challenging, but it is also often expected to be hard and full of mindless exhaustion.

Certainly not many of us expect to be pampered for six weeks. Yet these traditions do continue worldwide, even in the modern industrialized cities of China and India, where women are given total care during the first six weeks after childbirth, more than at any other time in their adult lives. Women describe how they felt about this:

> After my 40 days I felt like a queen. I was rested and my skin was smooth and shiny from the massage. - *Somali mother*

> A woman who has just given birth is treated like royalty. - *Samoan mother*

While physically the mother is rested and at ease, mentally she is *nourished* by the emotional support of those around her, and by knowing that she is in an honoured role. In Mali it is said that birth is 'the women's war'. Although death rates for women from causes related to pregnancy or childbirth has declined in the places where access to skilled healthcare is possible, giving birth is still an act marked by bravery and mental courage. Her status is acknowledged by the importance both Malian men and women place on 'the 40 days'.

Human beings are hard-wired to respond positively to an increase in status, and we respond negatively to a lowering of status, such as a perceived threat to our self-esteem or negative judgement on our performance.[1] When we are stressed, the levels of the hormone cortisol rise in our bodies. During the stress of giving birth and the immediate aftermath, cortisol naturally rises, making us more vulnerable to judgements of our status. By honouring the mother, supporting her new role and enabling her to feel proud of herself, her status in the family and the community is raised and her stress response is lowered. The way is thus smoothed for her to recover, bond with her baby and establish breastfeeding.

Bonding

The first weeks after birth are crucial ones for every baby's development. This is when the bonds are formed between the mother and baby. The mother learns to understand the baby's communication signals and respond to the baby's needs and their attuning to one another gives the baby her first experience of trust, love and safety. This is the basis for her future kindness to others and the capacity for empathy which will grow as she gets older. The quality of care and support that the mother receives at this time enables her to focus more or less on her newborn and helps to determine if this 'tuning in' can blossom.

Although often described in popular media as a 'rush of love' occurring the moment the newborn is first held by his (tired but joyful) mother, it is not always in the moments after birth that bonding instantly happens. Women who do not 'fall in love' instantly on seeing their babies need not feel guilty: this process can take time. It can take many repetitions of close contact between the mother and baby for bonds to form – this is mainly through cuddling, snuggling, gazing, sniffing and holding close to feed or breastfeed. Research on abandonment after birth[2] has shown that the mother is less likely to abandon her baby after the birth once her milk has come in and the flow of oxytocin, the 'hormone of mother love', is well established. As oxytocin brings feelings of safety, warmth and trust in both the baby and mother, the mutual feelings build up. Babies learn that when they are stressed or uncomfortable they will be tended to, calmed and loved by their mother and a small number of other caregivers. Oxytocin is not a general love drug, however: it builds specific connections over time between the baby and his mother and the others who care for him consistently. Having good connections with his caregivers helps his ability to receive and give love with joy[3] and other human beings become a source of pleasure to him.

Bonding is for the whole family too. It is not just the mother, but also those who care for and cuddle the baby day after day that are bonded to him. It is very good for the baby to be loved by a small group of people. Some researchers have shown that babies survive better if an aunt or grandmother is also involved in looking after them, and it is obvious from mothers' own words that both mother and baby benefit from the care of older, experienced women, as well as loving partners and family.

The quality of bonding has long-term effects on the growth of the baby's brain:

> The development of the baby's brain hinges on a complex interplay between the genes she was born with and the experiences her parents surround her

> with. In the first three years of life, in particular, there are critical periods during which her brain is "wired" through the sensing pathways of touch, vision, hearing, taste, and smell... Holding a newborn closely, gently stroking him as he is being fed, singing to him as you rock him in your arms - all these interactions fill him with a range of sensory stimuli that build a sense of security that will shape his capacity to establish warm, healthy relationships for the rest of his life.[4] – *Mary Gordon, Roots of Empathy (2009), p.211*

Having a strong bond between mother and baby is one of the most important benefits of caring well for the mother during her Golden Month. A stressed, sick, depressed or exhausted mother is in various degrees an absent mother from the baby's point of view.

Healing

Lastly, although this idea is not so common in Western thinking, by taking a six-week break to care for herself at this crucial time in her life the mother lays a foundation of good health for the future.

In many African traditions, women feel that having a good rest and being well cared for after birth is the reason for their continued strength and high fertility, even after many subsequent pregnancies.

> Usually a mother spends three to six months in recovery from the birth. If the birth was complicated even a year may be permitted. With each new pregnancy the rest period may increase if she needs

it. This means she is strong even after a lot of children.
– *Gabonese mother*

The power of this time to heal old illnesses is one reason that the month is called 'golden' in China.[5] It is one of the 'three golden opportunities' in Chinese medicine, when women can actively improve their health in the long term. (The other two are menstruation and the menopause.) East Asian traditions, as we saw earlier, like to think of birth as a watershed. During this massive life change, the potential exists to powerfully influence the energy, and therefore one's health, either positively or negatively. The strong movement of qi (vital force/energy) and blood during birth has allowed toxins to be expelled with the blood and body fluids and provoked an emotional opening, along with the physical surrender to the birth process. After birth, especially of the first baby, the entire nature of the body and the energy, the metabolism, the blood, nutrients and body fluids have reached a cusp, or 'peak of change', and are therefore easy to influence. The mother is now 'swept clean' in her body and psyche and is open to renewal.

At this moment, a good Oriental medicine practitioner takes the opportunity to begin a suitable treatment to eliminate old diseases as well as to establish the foundations for an improved state of health for the mother. In general, chronic diseases take a long time to treat because it takes time to build up treatment to a point where the patient is at the 'peak of change'. In the weeks directly after giving birth, however, a peak of change already exists, and a quick recovery from old disease can be achieved with skilful treatment. In general this involves encouraging the healthy discharge of old blood, warming the qi, strengthening qi and blood through a proper diet and herbal medicine tonics, resting, and supporting the abdominal organs. There is a rule which says 'three days of purgation, 30 days of tonification'. This means for the first three days after the birth the discharge of old blood is encouraged[6] and for the following 30 days the mother is given treatment to support her energy (qi) and blood and the restoration of her jing (essence).

This is the East Asian tradition, but even without the expertise of an Oriental medicine practitioner to give individualized treatment, following the basic ideas of good care that are discussed in Chapter Three involves these same principles, if described differently in different traditions. When the mother is cared for properly and she has a good experience in her Golden Month, it is believed she can be healed on many levels, from old illnesses, to traumatic experiences around previous births or postpartum experiences.

> I have always believed that Golden Month can change a woman's body condition. I took my Golden Month very seriously and at the end of it I felt really replenished and nourished... I used to get real bad period pains – they have totally disappeared now, after my Golden Month. I feel much stronger and healthier compared to before I had kids. – *Phoebe, mother of two, originally from Shanghai*

From the perspective of neuroscience, oxytocin, our 'love drug', again plays a major part in this healing and renewal. Oxytocin is a neuromodulator in the brain which can bring about lasting changes in the connections between nerve synapses.[7] As we saw earlier, oxytocin reinforces bonding and creates warmth and trust between mother and baby. When it is released, existing connections between neurons 'melt away' so that large-scale, long-term changes in the brain can follow. According to Walter Freeman, a professor in neuroscience at UC Berkeley, USA, oxytocin works to unlearn old patterns of thinking and memory and makes it possible to learn new patterns through the process of dissolving feelings of separation and distress. The security engendered by intense, loving, warm feelings frees us to learn new things, create new bonds and reconfigure old bonds. At no other time is oxytocin produced so intensely and enduringly than during childbirth and in the postpartum. When an oxytocin-rich environment is created by nurturing and caring for the mother, enabling her to relax, breastfeed, and spend time loving her baby, there is a tremendous capacity for healing.

***

1. R. Wilkinson and K. Pickett. *The Spirit Level: Why Equality is Better for Everyone* (Penguin, 2010), p.40.

2. M. Szalavitz and B. D. Perry. *Born for Love: Why Empathy is Essential - and Endangered* (William Morrow, 2010).

3. Ibid., p.132.

4. M. Gordon. *Roots of Empathy: Changing the World Child by Child* (Thomas Allen, 2009), p.211.

5. X. Zhao. *Reflections of the Moon on Water: Traditional Chinese Medicine for Women* (Vintage Press, 2006), p.186.

6. A commonly used formula to promote healthy discharge of blood after birth is *Sheng Hua Tang*, or 'generation and transformation decoction'. It consists of Angelicae Sinensis Radix, Persicae Semen, Ligustici Wallichii Radix, Glycyrrhizae Uralensis Radix Preparatae and Zingiberis Officinalis Rhizome. It is modified to suit each individual woman.

7. N. Doidge. *The Brain that Changes Itself* (Scribe Publications, 2010).

Chapter Three

The Ingredients for Good Care

Throughout the world women have always cared for each other after childbirth, giving practical help with housework and caring for older children, and providing care to the mother herself.[1] What is good care? When I spoke with women from Africa, Asia, the Pacific, Europe and South America I was surprised, again and again, at how much the traditions of each of these women had in common with each other. What emerged were four components of good care that they felt were the most important: rest, special diet, massage and warmth, and social support which included 'mothering the mother' and honouring her status. This chapter focuses on the first, more practical or concrete ingredients in this mix. The following chapter addresses the more social and emotional sides of good postpartum care for mothers.

Before progressing further, I feel I should mention the mothers who are reading this and haven't been able to do a Golden Month. They may feel they haven't fully recovered from giving birth or regained their energy, months or even years afterwards. Fortunately, if you are one of these women, there are options you can follow to retrieve some benefit. You can take time out, slow down, and consciously work on strengthening your health as a priority. Even though the Golden Month is irreplaceable, an awareness of what it contains can help you to choose a health recovery pathway that will suit you and support your healing.

I will now look at each of the healing components in turn, including some recipes for special foods prepared for mothers in the weeks after giving birth.

Rest

Giving birth is sometimes compared to running a marathon. We complete both of these tests of endurance triumphant and exhausted, but birth has unique demands on the body and mind that go beyond a marathon. As we discussed in Chapter One, enormous physical and hormonal changes take place when giving birth, including blood loss and the shock of pain. The uterus takes six weeks to heal and the output of the heart takes almost a month to rise back to normal. These changes alone need six weeks of convalescence.

But in addition, immediately after the birth there are a whole new set of physical and emotional demands on the mother. Firstly, she begins to produce milk and this uses a lot of qi and blood (in the Chinese medical sense). One old midwife used to tell her new mothers, 'You are going down the mines to the coal face now,' as their milk came in. Lactation demands more of the mother's energy than any other stage of reproduction: her energy requirements increase by 25–30%.[2] She must also adapt to new patterns of sleep which are in tune with the baby's, and this usually involves waking in the night. Finally, with all this she is developing an intense, loving relationship with a new individual in her life. It seems apparent that she doesn't need to do anything beyond the job description of her new role.

In practice this means that at first the mother needs to have total rest in quiet, unhurried surroundings. She sleeps when the baby sleeps and whenever she needs to sleep herself. She has a 'honeymoon' with her baby, and they lie around together in close skin-to-skin contact, bonding and breastfeeding.

> Once I left the hospital my sister-in-law fed me correctly and allowed me to have 40 days of rest... All I had to do was give breast milk to the baby, eat and sleep. – *Kadjiatou, Mali*

In the Chinese tradition, immediately following the birth of the baby the mother is advised not to read a lot or watch TV. She is encouraged not to focus her mind too much. Mental activity uses up a lot of qi, or vital energy, which she needs to conserve as much as possible at this moment.

Gradually she starts to exercise a little, as she feels ready. Only gentle exercise is advised, just walking for a short while, for example, or some yoga stretches.

There are two good reasons for this. Firstly, the energy is being used for healing at this moment. In Chinese medicine, jing (essence) is gradually being replenished and while this is happening, only the absolute minimum amount of energy needed for daily use is withdrawn from the now depleted reserves of jing. Any vigorous exercise takes qi and blood to support the muscles, diverting them away from their main role in maintaining the function of the internal organs and in healing.

Many women are afraid that if they don't exercise after giving birth they will gain weight, or not get back to their normal weight. This worry is unnecessary: when the body needs to recover, resting will not cause weight gain. On the contrary, it is the chronic stress that comes with *not* resting enough that causes weight gain, due to abnormal cortisol levels and adrenal fatigue.

A lack of rest during the six-week recovery period of the postpartum creates physical stress on the mother. This means the adrenals cannot normalize after the birth and the body stays in a 'fight or flight mode'. In other words, cortisol levels remain chronically high, eventually resulting in adrenal fatigue. Apart from weight gain, feelings of exhaustion in the morning and feeling 'wired' and unable to sleep at night are classic symptoms of this state. In Chinese medicine, it is said that a lack of rest causes the jing to be drained instead of being replenished. This is a serious situation because jing is the basis of all yin and yang, all activity and quiescence, in the body, and it means these aspects of our being are no longer being supported.

The second reason for restricting oneself to gentle exercise is that the ligaments are still soft from the effects of raised hormones in pregnancy and so the joints in the body need extra protection to prevent them from being damaged. In many traditions the hips are bound with a cloth, which is to help the joints stabilize as well as keeping the lower abdomen warm. This helps protect the body from ongoing backache and hip problems, a very common occurrence.

Sex is avoided for six weeks after birth. In traditional Māori culture, women were traditionally placed under *tapu*, or restriction, associated with a sacred status after birth. In Mali, the 40 days is specifically a time of abstinence. There are obvious good medical and social reasons for this. The sexual organs are healing and need to be rested, and there is also a risk of infection with sexual intercourse. The mother needs to conserve energy and focus on her baby. The prolactin she produces for lactation ensures that the hormones related to activity of the ovaries are suppressed, and they need to stay that way. Prolactin thus tends to suppress sexual desire. However, if sexual desire is provoked, the hormonal balance can be disrupted in favour of the ovaries. Desire also arouses strong emotions, and these can easily disturb the mind when it is vulnerable after giving birth. In the past, to avoid sex at this time, tradition would ensure that the husband and wife were physically separated after she had given birth; nowadays, however, both partners need to internalize a sexual separation during the postpartum, and this requires that both have a clear understanding of the mother's need to avoid sex. It is at the end of the postpartum, and after the mother feels fully recovered, that there is time for sex again. At this point the focus of healing can turn more towards the recovery of perineal and vaginal tone, and women can ease back into sexual relations again when they feel ready.

In France, from around two months after the birth, the government pays for 10–20 sessions of 'perineal re-education' for the mother. This is a heartening recognition of the support that may be needed to re-establish sexual relations, especially if there has been damage to the perineum.

After the rest period women are not expected to rush straight back to the responsibilities of their lives, but to slowly resume their household tasks, work, etc. as they feel able. It is still important to rest when they feel the need to, and some women from African countries such as Gabon and Ethiopia will traditionally be given six months of rest or more, if they need it. It is important also, since jing is depleted with age and continued childbearing, that older mothers and those with many children pay special attention to resting and recovering. They should not try to compete with younger women and should wait until they feel fully recovered before they return to normal duties.

Massage and warmth

In most traditions of Asia, the Pacific and Africa, mothers are massaged after birth, usually daily. Massage is very valuable as a passive form of exercise: without the mother using any of her own energy, her circulation is stimulated and she gets the pleasure and sense of well-being that comes with exercise. The circulation tends to be relatively slow after childbirth. This is because the body is resting and less mobile, the flow of blood is slower because the heart is pumping less blood with each beat, and the levels of proteins in the blood that help it to clot (blood-clotting factors) are still raised for some time after the birth. It is obviously very important to avoid blood clots, so maintaining good circulation through massage is extremely useful while the mother is resting.

Massage is usually given over the entire body, however certain areas are given special attention. There is some emphasis on the breasts to help the milk flow and stop blockages, but the main focus is on the lower abdomen. Bringing a good supply of blood to this area helps to heal the underlying reproductive organs and restore the muscle tone of the belly. Puja, an Indian mother who talks about her postpartum experiences in Chapter Five, describes how a strong Ayurvedic (Indian traditional medicine) massage given daily on her lower abdomen was able to remove the sensation of emptiness she had experienced there after the birth of her son, and restore a feeling of strength.

Different traditions use their own techniques to centre and strengthen the energy in the lower abdomen. In Vietnam a special massage is given after birth which coordinates the mother's breathing with the gentle movement of the massage therapist as she strokes down the front of the woman's body towards her uterus. The intention is to help return the energy to where it is said to originate, in the lower abdomen where the jing or essence is stored. The mother inhales as the therapist strokes downward and exhales as the hands are lifted off her belly before the next downward stroke, when she inhales again. This movement is repeated for up to half an hour.

While massage gives the new mother the opportunity to relax and enjoy the nurturing quality of human touch, when it is given regularly it is also able to promote circulation and healing, and strengthen the body and mind. For many women it is an indispensable part of their care after birth.

Ina, one of Ngangouma's granddaughters in Mali, had an unplanned pregnancy at the age of sixteen while she was still at high school. She remembers how crucial her daily massage was in helping her to cope with her situation:

> After I gave birth to my daughter I did not have the opportunity to do 'the 40 days' even though my high school said I should. My parents were upset with me and I was obliged to continue school for the sake of my education. The daily massage from my mother was what made me feel strong enough to cope. I could not have done without it.

Massage is always applied with warmth. If oil is used, it is heated first. In some cultures the mother is washed with a hot infusion of herbs before her massage, or, as in Gabon for example, she may be massaged with hot towels instead of with oil.

Indian Ayurvedic medicine is another tradition where massage is a highly developed routine in postnatal care. Here the 40 day rest period includes a daily massage which begins on day three after the delivery if it has been normal or after ten days in the case of caesarean section, or once the healing of the scar is stable. The practice of postnatal care and giving postnatal massage in India is very old, 5000–6000 years, and the techniques used also date back this far. In modern India massage continues to be practiced throughout the country and therapists offer 'package deals' of 40 days of massage after childbirth (although recently this is sometimes reduced to a 21-day deal in the fast-paced big cities). The therapist usually takes on two or three clients at a time, spending three hours with each mother per day massaging the baby, then the mother and then finally bathing the mother.

The massage given is very specific. Its aim is to both strengthen energy and encourage good circulation over the whole body, but particularly the uterus. Treatment and care in this 40-day period must re-establish the balance of *vata*, the energy which resides in the lower abdomen. The focus of the massage is therefore very much on the lower abdomen and the sacrum. The energy of vata requires warming methods of care and therefore hot oils are used and massage is followed by a hot wash or bath to ease out any toxins, even in hot weather. After this the mother must drink plenty of warm (not cold) water. A variety of heated oils can be chosen whose 'nature' is also more or less hot; this can modify the degree of heating she receives, although the overall effect should be warm. For example, mustard seed oil or sweet almond oils are chosen if the mother feels very cold, whereas if she is naturally quite hot coconut oil may be used. Massage begins on the back, as this is the most stressed area of the body and a common site of pain after childbirth, particularly the lower back. Beginning in this way has an immediate calming effect. The limbs are then massaged. The therapist massages the breasts in order to prevent engorgement and blockages, and then focuses on the lower abdomen, using deep circular strokes to gather the energy inward towards the centre of the body and upward. This technique draws energy in and encourages its circulation. Massage concludes on the head, using bhringaraj oil[3] which relaxes and reduces anger/depression and the hair loss which is common after childbirth. Overall the massage technique is quite deep, although the pressure is less on smaller, lighter women, and includes the rubbing of 107 neuromuscular junction points. Most women feel sleepy and relaxed after finishing the massage and bath, whereupon their lower abdomen is firmly bound with a light cloth and they can take the time to nap.

One important aspect of the massage is described by the Sanskrit word *snehan*. This means 'massage with love'. Simply touching with love, care and respect sends a message of love which enters the tissues of the body and helps to rebalance vata. It also lubricates the tissues and helps them release toxins.[4]

Mother warming

Warming the body is also an important way of caring for the mother. Warmth promotes the release of oxytocin (while cold stimulates adrenaline and suppresses oxytocin), so during the postpartum it is beneficial to receive warmth as a treatment, as well as to keep the body warm generally. When the body is depleted, as it is after labour, it becomes easily chilled. To remedy this, there are a number of different methods of warming the mother, usually concentrated on her lower abdomen. In China, for example, 'mother warming' is performed around one week after delivery, using the technique of moxibustion. A lighted cigar-like stick of the herb mugwort is held over the skin at a comfortable height and passed up and down along the midline of the lower abdomen between the pubic bone and the navel, and then along the lower back between the waist and the tailbone. The treatment takes five to ten minutes on each side. Mother warming is usually given a week after the birth, if there are no complications. If there has been a caesarean section it is given after two weeks, since the position of the uterus normalizes more slowly after surgery. It is not performed if there is fever or other signs of heat, such as night sweating. In general, 'mother warming' treatment is warming and soothing and it strengthens the jing. It can be quite powerful in quickly boosting the energy and sense of well-being.

In many cultures the body is kept warm, even in hot climates, by wrapping a scarf or towel around the waist and hips until the mother feels she has recovered. Firmly wrapping in the area of the reproductive organs warms them and helps them recover their tone. Keeping the waist and hips warm also supports the kidneys and adrenals, and once more, helps to restore jing. Some traditions combine several methods of warming.

As part of a three-month rest period after she gave birth to her son, Anjalika, from Sri Lanka, was given a warming treatment every day. Her treatment began with a 'smoking', where she stood over the smoke from the embers of burnt garlic skin, castor oil plant and coconut shells. This smoke is antiseptic and healing for the perineum and vagina. Then she lay down and was massaged with a warmed herbal cotton ball pressed over her lower back and hips. The cotton ball contained hot, steamed herbs which were wrapped in a fist-sized muslin ball.[5] Finally her hips were wrapped firmly with a cloth and she rested with a brazier of burnt coconut shells warming her feet. This treatment continued for a month. It was part of the overall care that her mother-in-law and father-in-law gave her, which she says she will never forget.

In cold countries the mother is also instructed to avoid draughts and cold air, and some mothers go so far as to stay in the house for the whole six-week postnatal period. Traditionally in China there were rules about not wetting the hair or exposing oneself to cold water. Even though this idea came from a time when women had long hair, and before there were hot showers, hair dryers and central heating, it is still important to protect the mother from catching a chill while her body is yang deficient, weakened and vulnerable. When qi is weak we are less protected from external influences than at normal times. One of the roles of qi is to protect the surface of the body by controlling the opening and closing of the pores - after childbirth this function is also weakened and the pores may remain too open, leaving the body at risk of being chilled by cold and wind.

Food for new mothers

The essentials of a good postnatal diet are founded in food which is nutrient-dense. This means food in its natural state which is a concentrated source of the necessary vitamins, minerals, healthy fats, proteins and complex carbohydrates.[6] - *Loula George*

Dietary therapy is a potent method of healing the body, and good postpartum nutrition can make an enormous difference to the experience a mother has in her Golden Month and her ability to recover well. Bearing in mind the increased nutritional requirements during recovery and breastfeeding, the type of diet that is necessary is nutrient-dense. Dietary principles for the postpartum are surprisingly similar around the world, in spite of different terminology, culinary traditions and foods available. While we talk about nutrient-dense food, Ethiopian women talk about 'strong' food, and in China the postpartum diet nourishes 'yin, blood and qi'. What is consistent between the various cultures and locations is the *type* of foods mothers eat and the *way* they eat them. These relate specifically to the needs of the body after delivery.

There are three main requirements from the diet after delivery: to replace lost blood and nutrients, to repair damaged tissue and heal the uterus and vagina, and to support breastfeeding. There is a simple fourth requirement also, which is that food provides a source of warmth for the body.

For the first three requirements, good-quality protein and carbohydrates are needed. I will first look at the importance of protein in the postnatal diet. In Eastern medical traditions, protein builds yin and blood, and strong blood of the Heart is said to be the basis of a good shen, or spirit, which as we have already seen, needs special nurturing after childbirth. Therefore protein is said to be not only a building block for the body and mind, but also an emotionally 'grounding' type of food. In Western traditions protein is a nutrient-dense food which is the basis of sustained energy, and cellular nourishment and repair. Protein is particularly nourishing if eaten in the form of bone broths, because in this form it contains many minerals and other nutrient-rich substances which have leached from the bones and gristle. One of the primary postnatal foods are therefore bone-based soups, and it is interesting to find that worldwide, from the Amazon to China to Scotland, chicken, beef or fish soup is a favourite in the traditional postnatal diet.

Many of the mineral requirements of the postnatal diet such as iron, calcium and magnesium are also met by using bone stock as the basis of soups, stews and risottos, etc. Chicken stock deserves a special mention. It is tasty, digestible, cheap, and easy to make, and it has its own outstanding properties. The carcass of a chicken is made of bones, cartilage and tendons which, when boiled to make stock, release many minerals in a form which is easy to absorb, as well as amino acids. The stock also contains substances which feed and repair the gut wall whose health is important for both the nervous and immune systems, and the marrow from the bones contains immunoglobulins which give immune support. In Chinese medicine the properties of chicken are warm and sweet, and as such, it strengthens the qi and the blood, benefits the digestion, and supports lactation. In Western terms chicken soup supports the nervous and immune systems, reduces allergies, improves digestion, relaxes, soothes and strengthens. It fully deserves its reputation as a cure-all and its label as 'Jewish penicillin'.

All bone stocks contain gelatin which should be thought of as a 'super food' and is ideal for a postnatal diet. Gelatin in Chinese medicine is a warming blood tonic which helps prevent excessive uterine bleeding. It contains glycine and proline which are amino acids found in bones, organs and fibrous tissue. These substances are anti-inflammatory and support the immune system, weight regulation and the healthy growth of skin, hair, nails and joints. They also help improve sleep. The amount of glycine and proline is often inadequate in the modern diet as we do not eat as much bone-based soup, offal, or gristle and bone as our ancestors used to. Jellied food, which uses gelatin as its base, has also gone out of fashion.

Chicken stock

Chicken soup has many variations worldwide. Some recipes prepared for postnatal mothers include tonic herbs and some add herbs to promote lactation. Here is a basic stock which you might like to use to enhance the nutrient capacity of soups, stews, risottos and any other dish you care to make which requires liquid. Note that acids like vinegar or lemon juice are added to the stock to help leach the minerals from the bones.

1 *free-range* or *organic chicken*, fat glands and gizzard removed, feet optional (the feet are high in gelatin so you may want to keep them in the soup)

1 large *onion*

2 *carrots*

3 *celery sticks*

1 bunch *parsley*

Water to cover

2 Tbsp *cider vinegar* or *lemon juice*

Cut chicken into pieces. Roughly chop the onion, carrots, celery and parsley. Add all ingredients to a large saucepan or stock pot. Bring to the boil and simmer for at least two hours; the longer you let it simmer, the richer the flavour will be. Remove from the heat, strain out the bones and vegetables and let cool. Skim off the fat when cool and store in the refrigerator for up to three days, or alternatively, freeze in portions to defrost and reheat as required.

Variations

Here are some common variations of chicken soup from China, with herbs added according to the mother's needs.

Follow the basic chicken stock recipe but leave out the lemon juice or cider vinegar and add the herbs shown below. Simmer for one to two hours, as per the basic stock recipe.

1 This is an important recipe to tonify the qi and strengthen yin and blood. Combine the following herbs in a pot with the chicken and water:

30g *huang qi* (Astragali Radix)
30g *dang shen* (Codonopsis Radix)
10g *dang gui* (Angelicae Sinensis Radix)
30g *shan yao* (Dioscoreae Rhizome)
30g *yu zhu* (Polygonati Odorati Rhizome)
15 pieces *da zao* (Jujubae Fructus)

Also add a little *ground black pepper*, a few slices of *fresh ginger root*, chopped *spring onion*, a little *white wine* and season with *salt* to taste.

2 This variation is particularly useful to help the uterus return to a normal position after childbirth and helps strengthen the lower back. Combine the following ingredients in a pot with the chicken and water:

30g *du zhong* (Eucommia Cortex)
few slices of *fresh ginger*
few drops of *white wine*

3 This recipe is popular in Taiwan. It has quite a warming effect. Combine the following ingredients in a pot with the chicken and water:

a little *sesame oil*
salt to taste
fresh ginger
spring onion

4 This variation is especially good for mothers with a weak digestion as well as poor lactation. Combine the following ingredients in a pot with the chicken and water:

30g *huang qi* (Astragali Radix)
15g *dang shen* (Codonopsis Radix)
15g *shan yao* (Dioscoreae Rhizome)
15 pieces *da zao* (Jujubae Fructus)
a little *yellow rice wine*

5 This variation is sweet in taste and its action is to calm the mind. Combine the following ingredients in a pot with the chicken and water:

9g *long yan rou* (Longan Arillus)
few slices of *fresh ginger*

For vegetarians who are not obtaining their essential nutrients through bone-based soups or other animal proteins, one way of improving the density of nutrients is through sprouting grains, seeds and pulses. Sprouting increases protein and levels of vitamins B and C and carotene in the grains, and it neutralizes phytic acid (which inhibits the absorption of zinc, magnesium, iron and calcium). It also neutralizes the enzyme inhibitors which are found naturally in grains and which tend to inhibit our own digestive enzymes. Sprouting produces many enzymes that help digestion. These qualities make sprouted foods beneficial for all women to eat after childbirth, even if one is not vegetarian.

Good-quality carbohydrates are the basis of cellular function: they give energy, help raise serotonin (a 'feel-good' neurotransmitter) and, in Chinese medicine, are an important source of qi, or vital energy. After childbirth there is an increased need for energy, via carbohydrates, to produce breast milk, so it is not a good time to be cutting back on carbohydrates. The *type* of carbohydrate we eat, however, is crucial for our weight to remain normal and stable. Many women believe that their figures should spring back to normal as soon as possible after the birth, and so they eat very little and try to avoid eating carbohydrates. They may also start exercising too early for the same reason (to lose weight), and the combination of these two factors means their milk production can go down. Carbohydrates themselves do not pose a problem for weight gain. It is when carbohydrates are 'empty', in the sense that they contain no nutrients, only calories, that there is a problem. Empty calories come from refined carbohydrates: refined flour and the sugars in pastries, cakes and biscuits, and these carbohydrates tempt us to keep on eating because the nutrients the body needs are not in them, so the body continues to crave more food. However if we are eating complex carbohydrates, from wholemeal flour, brown rice, etc., and including other nutrient-dense foods in our diet, then the desire to eat is less because we feel satisfied. People eat a greater volume when their food is nutrient deficient and this is where the risk of gaining weight lies. They are eating 'empty' calories.

Other than in bone-based soups, the essential postnatal minerals – iron, magnesium and calcium – are found in the following foods: iron is found in dried fruit (figs, dates, raisins, apricots), dark leafy greens, beans and peas, almonds, brazil nuts, sesame seeds, peanuts, blackstrap molasses, brewer's yeast, parsley, kelp and whole grains (especially sprouted); magnesium is in leafy greens, seeds and nuts; and calcium is also found in seeds and nuts, especially almonds and sesame, as well as dairy products and dark green, leafy vegetables.

One of the most important minerals in the postpartum diet is zinc. Zinc needs to be given special attention as it is commonly depleted by modern diet and lifestyles, and therefore women often begin their pregnancy with low levels of zinc. Zinc supports mood, appetite and a well-functioning reproductive system. The pill, fertility drugs, miscarriage, surgery, illness and stress, sugars and refined carbohydrates, and even the pesticides used on fruit and vegetables all contribute to the depletion of zinc in the body. The requirements for zinc also rise during periods of 'nutritional stress' on the body, such as in pregnancy, and even more so while breastfeeding.[7]

Other changes in our bodies during labour and delivery also make us susceptible to low zinc levels. In a normal situation the placenta is full of zinc. During pregnancy the body's levels of copper, an antagonist of zinc, are doubled: after the placenta is discharged, and with it the high levels of zinc along with other minerals, there is a relative imbalance of zinc in favour of copper. A low level of zinc is, in itself, a risk factor for depression, but if zinc levels have not been adequate during pregnancy there is now a situation where copper can easily rise out of proportion to zinc levels, to the point where the symptoms of a relative copper excess can manifest. These include anxieties, phobias and depression. So while a pregnancy ideally begins with good zinc levels in the mother, women also need to have their levels monitored during pregnancy, and should quickly supplement zinc before the birth if their levels are low. Good dietary sources of zinc include seafood, pumpkin, sesame and sunflower seeds, almonds, fresh ginger, wheat germ and leafy greens.

This leads to an important point. In order to maximize our chances of having a good postnatal experience (and healthy baby), there are three stages of nutritional support that we need to pay attention to: before conception, during pregnancy, and after birth. Before conception, a good diet helps to support and strengthen the jing and the nutrients in our blood. Besides the benefits to the mother, the egg, whose quality is determined by the mother's jing, and the embryo are more likely to be healthy and vigorous if there is good maternal nutrition.

Egg quality is determined by the number of 'batteries' that provide its energy stores. The batteries are analogues of tiny organelles called 'mitochondria' which are the energy producers of our cells. As we age, or if we are nutrient deficient or filled with toxins, the energy-producing capacity of the mitochondria decreases. The egg is connected to the circulation prior to ovulation and is connected again after implantation, when the embryo is able to continue getting nutrients through the mother's developing placenta, but during the seven days between ovulation and implantation the dividing embryo is dependent on the energy coming from the mitochondria which were in the egg at the time of ovulation. If the embryo 'runs out of batteries' and stops dividing, implantation may not take place. It is therefore very important to increase the energy stores (jing) to an egg prior to ovulation. Once the embryo has implanted, it is nourished by what comes through the bloodstream of the mother, via the placenta. For example, the baby emerges from the womb with an immature gut and brain: if the mother takes fish oil and a probiotic (or probiotic-rich food) during pregnancy, these functions will be supported from the beginning, giving the baby's brain and digestion a good start at birth.

For mothers themselves, there is good evidence that a 'health-conscious' diet in pregnancy can reduce postnatal depression. In 2011 a team of researchers in Crete, Greece, showed that pregnant women who ate the classic Mediterranean diet which is rich in vegetables, fruits, fish and seafood, dairy products, pulses, locally produced extra virgin olive oil (up to 40g daily) and nuts, were about 50% less likely to have high levels of postpartum depressive symptoms than their counterparts who ate a 'Western' type of diet which consisted of meat and meat products, sugar and sweets, fats except olive oil, sauces and beverages, cereals, eggs, salty snacks and potatoes. These latter foods tend to create oxidative stress, leading to inflammation which is, in turn, associated with depression. An increase in sugary products alone showed a correlation with higher rates of postpartum depressive symptoms.[8] All of the healthy food groups in the Mediterranean diet were rich in antioxidants, which protect against oxidative stress.

At a fundamental level, it also makes sense to have good nutrient status before beginning arduous work like labour and birth. It is much better to start the postpartum with all resources in place, than to try and build them up from low levels after giving birth, as this can take time.

Finally, adequate levels of fats are important in the postnatal diet. Breast milk is fatty and the breastfeeding mother needs to keep up with the demand on her body to produce milk by eating healthy fats. In fact, not only breast-feeding mothers – fats and cholesterol are also important in the manufacture of hormones as well as in brain health.[9] Healthy fats, such as unprocessed olive oil, tend to have strong antioxidant properties, and are high in omega-3 fatty acids. Good sources of omega-3s are also fish and fish oil, wild and grass-fed game, and flaxseed oil. However, overindulging in fats, especially in rich, creamy or fried foods, overloads the digestive process, interferes with hormone production and leads to weight gain. Fried and processed food, such as takeaways, potato crisps, and margarines all contain the trans fats which create oxidative stress and have an inflammatory effect on the body and brain.

The fourth requirement, you may recall, is that food eaten in the weeks after birth should provide a source of warmth for the body. A simple way for this to be met is for food to be eaten warm or hot. Warmth supports the circulation and the movement of blood to areas which need healing, or, in the case of the breasts, need to produce milk. If all of these four requirements are met through a good intake of protein, minerals and carbohydrates, and food and drinks are taken warm, the body is well supported to recuperate and breastfeed.

However, it is also true that the benefits we can get from food are only as good as the strength of our digestion. In Chinese medicine, the digestion is the foundation of 'acquired' strength (post-heaven jing), that is, the energy we generate day to day, rather than what we have inherited. If the digestion is strong we can extract the greatest benefit from what we eat and establish a good basis for health and longevity. When the body is vulnerable after birth, special care needs to be taken not to damage the digestive function, and to actively support it through a correct diet. On the other hand, as many toxins are expelled with blood and body fluids at birth, in this 'cleansed' state after birth the mother can benefit to the maximum from a correct diet: at this moment good nutrition can be very effectively absorbed by the body.

So how can we strengthen the organs of digestion, especially when the body not only has to regain lost qi and blood, but has the additional task of transforming food into extra blood to make milk? First of all, the stomach shouldn't have to work too hard. Grains should be well cooked and proteins cooked in casseroles or soups with plenty of liquid, so that the tissues are broken down and easy to assimilate. For the enzymes of digestion to be activated properly the food must also enter the stomach warm. If food is cold, not only does the body get chilled, but it has to work extra hard to raise the temperature in the stomach back to a point where enzymes can be active again. In doing so, it wastes precious energy unnecessarily. In addition, digestion may be incomplete because the enzymes have not been able to work efficiently, which means that even if the food is as fresh and nourishing as possible we will not get the full benefit from it. When the digestion is devitalized by cold there also tends to be bloating and sugar cravings.

Food is said to have a 'warm', 'hot', 'cool' or 'cold' nature in Chinese medicine. Warm-natured food helps to support the digestion and blood circulation, strengthen the qi and keep the body temperature warm, while cool- and cold-natured food will be cooling on the body and tend to cause contraction and congealing. However, hot-natured foods such as peppery spices are over-stimulating and overheating and should be avoided in the postpartum. There is an axiom from a famous classical text in Chinese medicine, which says: 'strong heat damages qi but mild warmth strengthens qi'.[10] So when it comes to the nature of a particular food, the distinguishing between warm and hot is important. It is true that each individual has a need for different degrees of warmth according to their body constitution, which is a subject too big for discussion here, but in general after birth the body must overall have warm-natured foods since it is in a state of relative qi deficiency in all women. Some examples of foods which are warm in nature and which act as tonics for the qi are oats, rice, kumara (sweet potato), yams, mushrooms, cinnamon, dill, fennel, fenugreek, ginger, nutmeg, rosemary and thyme. Those which are warm in nature and nourish blood are chicken soup, bone-based soup, corn, sweet rice, beetroot, dark leafy greens, apricots, avocado, dates, sesame seeds, kidney beans, spinach and red meat.

Fermented foods deserve a mention for their importance in supporting digestion. Fermented foods have always been an important part of traditional dietary practices around the world because of their ability to populate the intestines with healthy bacteria which support the immune, nervous and digestive systems, as well as the production of B vitamins. They contain enzymes which support digestion. The fermented foods of our forebears helped to keep them healthy and energized, and these are good reasons to include them in the postnatal diet. Lately, however, the eating of fermented foods has declined in the general population, and it is hard to start a new eating practice immediately after giving birth. At this point we can look back through our family history, ask what our grandmothers ate and follow our traditions. We can begin with the fermented foods we are familiar with. In East Asia, for example, there is fish sauce and pickled vegetables, in Europe it is yoghurt and sauerkraut and pickles, in Africa it is fermented fish and soured milk.

There is often controversy about the benefit of using raw foods, which tend to be cool in 'nature' (from a Chinese medical perspective) in a diet which emphasizes warmth as one of its fundamental principles to aid good digestion and recovery. Raw foods such as cold-pressed extra virgin olive oil, dates, figs, raw honey, mangoes, kiwifruit, pineapple and sprouted grains and seeds are high in enzymes which aid digestion. Therefore if they are used in moderation, they can support the overall aim of the postnatal diet, and if they are taken simultaneously with warm food and drinks so that they arrive in the stomach warm, they will be the most beneficial. Having warm soup or casserole with a green salad, for example, combines the benefits of the vitamins found in fresh vegetables with the warmth and dense nutrients of the soup.

Here is a postnatal menu from Sri Lanka, courtesy of Anjalika. It combines raw and cooked ingredients.

Kiri Anguna

This salad is said to be blood cleansing. Its main ingredient, kiri anguna[11] is used in Ayurvedic medicine to help in tissue repair. It contains many antioxidants which help prevent mastitis and other infections. The anguna leaves may be substituted with any leafy greens.

2 handfuls of *kiri anguna leaves*, finely chopped

½ cup of fresh, grated *coconut*

Pepper, salt and *lime juice* to taste

Optional: a little *green chilli* and *red onion*, finely chopped

Combine all ingredients in a bowl.

Kiri Cos

This dish promotes a good milk supply. The young jackfruit may be substituted with either dried or tinned jackfruit.

Coconut oil for cooking

A small pinch of *mustard seeds*

4–5 *black peppercorns*

1 small *cinnamon stick*

1 *red onion* or 5–6 *shallots*, finely chopped

2 *cloves garlic*, finely chopped

1 *fresh green chilli*, seeds removed and finely chopped (optional)

1 *dried chilli*, finely chopped

A few *curry leaves*, fresh or dried

1 tsp *turmeric*

1 *tomato*, chopped

10 cloves from a *young firm jackfruit*, not quite ripe

2 cups *coconut milk*

Salt to taste

Heat a little oil in a pan. Add the mustard seeds to the pan and cook until they pop. Reduce the heat and add the peppercorns and cinnamon stick with the onion, garlic, chillis and curry leaves and until lightly brown. Add turmeric and chopped tomato and cook to a paste. Add the jackfruit with enough water to cover them, and simmer until soft. Add the coconut milk and salt to taste. Cook a further 5 minutes, uncovered.

Miri Smalo (river fish curry) with Red Rice

This a well-known recipe eaten throughout Sri Lanka for recovery after childbirth. It is eaten with a salad of anguna leaves, but any salad of leafy greens may be substituted.

Pinch of *mustard seeds*

Oil for cooking

2 slices *fresh ginger*

2 cloves *garlic*, finely chopped

1 *onion*, finely chopped

3cm piece of *cinnamon stick*

Pinch of *curry leaves*

1 tsp *fresh chilli*, chopped

½ tsp *turmeric*

2 Tbsp *tamarind paste*

1 tsp *cumin seeds* and 1 tsp *coriander seeds*, roasted and ground with salted water to make a paste

1 *freshwater fish*, cleaned and cut into chunks

Fry mustard seeds in a little oil until they pop. Add ginger, garlic, onion, cinnamon stick, curry leaves and chilli, and sauté mixture until lightly brown. Stir in the turmeric.

Mix the tamarind paste with the cumin/coriander paste and add the fish pieces. Add this mixture to the pan and stir gently to coat fish with all ingredients. Add ½ cup hot water and bring to the boil. Reduce to a low heat and simmer until the fish is just cooked, stirring very gently once or twice so as not to break the pieces. Serve with steamed red rice.

Beyond the benefits to the mother's recovery after childbirth and her production of breast milk, there is another reason for the stomach to be well supported and functioning well. If food is too rich and not well digested, or if the digestion is weak, fat globules in the blood circulation can easily block the milk ducts and cause mastitis. In Chinese medicine this is explained by the fact that the 'channels' of the Stomach and Liver pass through the breast and therefore any congestion in these organs, either from excess or weakness, can cause blockage on the pathways of the channels.

Dietary tonics and the use of supplements

The mother's consumption of her placenta as a tonic after childbirth has been in the spotlight in Western countries recently. In Chinese medicine human placenta (ze he che) is classed as a very powerful medicinal tonic. Essentially it is warm in nature and strengthens most aspects of energy, including qi, blood and essence. Also, since both Heart blood and essence are at the root of spirit, it is said to strengthen and calm mind/spirit. It is described as the quintessential food to nourish post-heaven essence.[12] It contains oxytocin, vitamin B6, iron, endorphins which help cope with pain and enhance mood, a neurohormone called gonadotrophin-releasing hormone (GnRH) which decreases anxiety and fatigue, very high levels of corticotrophin-releasing hormone (CRH) which helps regulate the stress response and calm the mind, and hormones which help regulate thyroid function and lactation. It is also rich in zinc, an essential mineral for maintaining normal mood and appetite, as we saw earlier.

However some controversy surrounds the use of placenta. Historically in China it was classified as a 'galloping medicine' due to its particularly powerful effects and it wasn't given to postpartum mothers. It was generally prescribed as part of essence-tonifying formulae for men. Some mothers, indeed, have reported feeling wired and overwhelmed when taking it. In addition, as it acts as a filter for the baby during pregnancy, it may accumulate unwanted toxins.

Having said this, many women find that it does help them, particularly if it used in the short term. A small survey published in 2013 by two anthropologists and a placenta encapsulation provider found that a majority of mothers who consumed their own placenta in capsule form reported positive experiences, in particular improved mood and increased energy.[13] Without any real research to date to support its use, however, it is best to use placenta with caution and only on the advice of a Chinese medical practitioner.

A general programme of supplements which can be followed for six weeks after the birth would include fish oil, a good-quality probiotic, a good natal multivitamin and mineral supplement, and, if necessary, iron, zinc and B vitamins if these levels are low. The 'if necessary' is important to note. Taking supplements can be a potent therapy, and taking certain supplements when it is not necessary can unbalance metabolic functions in the body. For this reason, women should see a registered health professional to establish if and what nutritional deficiencies they might have before they choose a regime of supplements after giving birth.

There has been a lot of research into links between nutrition before, during and after pregnancy and mothers' mental health. Researchers at the University of Calgary Brenda Leung and Bonnie Kaplan published a review of studies done prior to 2009 and found strong evidence that an adequate intake of essential fatty acids, folate and iron protect against postpartum depression.[14, 15] DHA (found mainly in fish oil) is an especially important fatty acid. Joseph Hibbeln at the National Institutes of Health, Maryland, compared published reports of levels of DHA in mothers' milk, seafood consumption and levels of depression and found a correlation between lowered rates of postpartum depression and greater seafood consumption. In this study, higher levels of DHA in the breastmilk correlated with lower levels of postpartum depression.[16] The study of Cretan mothers which was discussed earlier shows that a diet during pregnancy which is high in antioxidants, essential fatty acids, vitamins, minerals and enzymes, and low in sugar and trans fats significantly lowers the risk of postpartum depression.

The way food is eaten can make a big difference to how it is digested and its ability to provide nourishment. The connection of food with love is known and felt by everyone: adults, children and babies, as soon as we are born, in fact! In traditions around the world, visitors come after the mother has given birth to congratulate her with gifts of special food and treats, whether it is a bunch of grapes, champagne and chocolates, or a brace of succulent game birds from the forest. During the Golden Month the benefits of a meal cooked and served by caring friends and relatives go far beyond its physical nutritional value. Eating together with friends and family raises oxytocin levels in everyone concerned, which in turn enhances relaxation and digestion. In Chinese medicine, we say that enjoying food brings additional qi, or vital energy, to the digestion, and this will hasten the mother's recovery. Enjoying food together benefits everyone's health and well-being, and it is worth taking the time for.

On a physical level, it is important after childbirth to eat in a way that does not overload the stomach or destabilize the blood sugar. This means eating frequent, small meals, chewed well and not gulped down, rather than two or three larger ones in a day. If there is too long between meals and blood sugar drops, the qi drops with it and the body goes into 'overdrive', drawing on its essence (jing), that precious substance which we are trying to conserve and replenish at this moment after childbirth. If meals are not being served as often as one would wish, having healthy snack foods at hand can be useful and is easy to plan.

> For the first four weeks after I gave birth I was shattered. I just ate and slept. I was so exhausted that even thinking about food was difficult. I was hungry because of breastfeeding and aware that I needed to eat well, but I couldn't think about exactly what to eat. I just wanted food and right now. Although for the evenings I had pre-prepared and frozen the meals, and friends brought some evening meals too, I was glad to have organized good snack foods for the daytime. - *Mary, 40-year-old mother, New Zealand*

Here is a recipe for a special snack food from Morocco that is eaten after fasting, and during the 40 days after childbirth. It is called 'Sellou', and this particular version comes from Casablanca, courtesy of Huria. Huria says,

> In Morocco we spoil the mother after she has given birth. She asks for Sellou and has it while she is feeding her baby. It is eaten in the morning and afternoon, between meals. It is very tasty and healthy, and anyone who eats it goes crazy for it. The dish of Sellou sits beside the mother and she

eats it with a little spoon while she is feeding. Throughout her 40 days of recovery, she eats the Sellou as a snack. It warms her body, gives her energy and helps to increase her milk supply. The mother also drinks tea from verbena leaves to help digestion, and stop colic in the baby, as well as fenugreek tea to boost milk supply.

Breakfast is the most important meal of the day. It is 'breaking the fast' and fuelling up after the night, and so it is energy-giving and sustaining. The digestive function is at its peak in the morning. On the Chinese 24-hour clock of energy cycles, between 7 a.m. and 9 a.m. is the time when the Stomach organ has most energy flowing through it. It is therefore a general principle of healthy eating to have the most substantial meal of the day early in the morning. This is especially so for the new mother if she is breastfeeding in the night. If mothers eat bigger meals in the morning and lunchtime, and a relatively smaller one at night, they generally feel much better and more able to cope because they are 'fuelled' for the day. And if they need to be fuelled during the night as well, as many mothers do, light food, such as a handful of almonds, or toast with honey, and warm drinks will satisfy hunger without overloading the digestion.

Sellou

500g *blanched almonds*

Olive oil for cooking

500g *brown sesame seeds* (brown seeds are richer in calcium than white)

1 Tbsp generously heaped *fennel seeds*

500g *flour* (spelt or stoneground wholemeal flour may be substituted)

1 crystal *gum Arabic*

A pinch of *white sugar*

1½ Tbsp generously heaped *cinnamon powder*

Good-quality *honey* to taste

250g–300g *butter*, melted
(the butter used traditionally is made at home from unpasteurized milk)

First prepare the dry ingredients. Fry the almonds on a low heat in a little olive oil, or bake in the oven until lightly brown, drain on kitchen paper, and then grind finely. Dry roast the sesame seeds for 5 minutes and then grind finely. Roast the fennel seeds and grind them to a powder. Dry roast the flour in a low oven for 1 hour, stirring often with a spoon, and finally, pound the crystal of gum Arabic into a fine powder with a pinch of white sugar.

Mix all the dry ingredients together by hand and then add honey and melted butter. Shape to form a cone or round hillock, as desired. This recipe will keep refrigerated for 20 days, although I have found it so popular with mothers that they are often on to their next batch of sellou well before that.

A final word should be said about drinking enough water. The general rules of good hydration apply here too, but with the increased demand for fluid while breastfeeding, it's important to be extra mindful of hydration. To keep the stomach functioning well and the body from getting chilled, drinks need to be warm, even when breastfeeding during the night. Simple herbal teas of fennel and dill are good to have on hand. They benefit lactation and the digestion of both mother and baby.

A good postpartum diet is relatively easy to achieve and is not expensive. The type of diet for the postpartum is a restorative diet which factors in the increased nutritional demands of recovery from childbirth, and lactation. It gives special attention to nutrient-rich food which is physically warm and also warming in its 'nature', and it emphasizes eating food which is prepared with love and care and enjoyed in a relaxed environment. The help and support of other people preparing food is a good example of the other main form of good postpartum care, best described as 'mothering the mother', and in the next chapter I will look at this aspect in more detail.

***

1. S. Pairman, S. Tracy, C. Thorogood and C. Pincombe et al. *Midwifery: Preparation for Practice.* 2nd edn (Churchill Livingston, 2010), p.589.

2. A. M. Prentice, C. J. Spaaij, G. R. Goldberg, et al. 'Energy Requirements of Pregnant and Lactating Women', *European Journal of Clinical Nutrition*, Feb. 1996; 60(supp.1): s82–s111.

3. Eclipta Alba steeped in sesame oil.

4. Dr Priya Punjabi. Private communication with the author, 2014.

5. The herbs used are pawata/Malabar nut (*Justicia adhatoda*), edaru/castor oil plant (*Ricinus communis*), nika/five-leaved chaste tree (*Vitex negundo*) and kaha/turmeric. These herbs have properties which warm, detoxify and promote blood circulation.

6. Loula George. Private communications with the author. The insights of naturopaths Loula George and Sheran Marra, leading specialists in fertility, pregnancy and maternal nutrition, have contributed to this section on diet.

7. N. F. Krebs. 'Zinc Supplementation During Lactation', *American Journal of Clinical Nutrition*, August 1998; 68(2 supp.): 509s–512s.

8. L. Chatzi, V. Melaki, K. Sarri, et al. 'Dietary Patterns During Pregnancy and the Risk of Postpartum Depression: The Mother-Child 'Rhea' Cohort in Crete, Greece'. *Public Health Nutrition*, 2011; 14(9): 1663–70.

9. J. R. Hibbeln. 'Seafood Consumption, the DHA Content of Mothers' Milk and Prevalence Rates of Postpartum Depression: A Cross-national Ecological Analysis', *Journal of Affective Disorders*, May 2002; 69(1–3): 15–29.

10. *Huang Di Nei Jing* [Yellow Emperor's Classic of Internal Medicine] Authors unknown. c. 500 BC.

11. *Wattakaka volubilis.*

12. D. Maxwell. 'The Clinical Utility of the Concept of Jing in Chinese Reproductive Medicine', *Journal of Chinese Medicine*, 2012; 98: p.61.

13. J. Selander, A. Cantor, S. M. Young, et al. 'Human Maternal Placentophagy: A Survey of Self-Reported Motivation and Experiences Associated with Placenta Consumption', *Ecology of Food and Nutrition*, 2013; 52(2): 93–115.

14. B. M. Leung and B. J. Kaplan. 'Perinatal Depression: Prevalence, Risks and the Nutritional Link - a Review of the Literature', *Journal of the American Dietary Association*, Sept. 2009; 109(9): 1566–75.

15. M. Fava and D. Mischoulon. 'Folate in Depression: Efficacy, Safety, Differences in Formulations and Clinical Issues', *Journal of Clinical Psychiatry*, 2009; 70(supp. 5): 12–17.

16. Hibbeln. 'Seafood Consumption, the DHA Content of Mothers' Milk and Prevalence Rates of Postpartum Depression'.

Chapter Four

Mothering Mothers

The supportive presence of caring others is the essential factor in carrying out all the other practices of the Golden Month. Mothering the mother is one of the most important aspects of good postnatal care.

> Giving birth is a wonderful gift but it hurts both the body and the heart. The job of the nannies (grandmothers/elders) is to help bring the mother back into 'consciousness' so that she can be a source of nourishment to her child. - *Wai Mason, New Zealand Māori from Tauranga Moana, kuia (respected elder and spiritual/community leader)*

Wai's statement expresses recognition of the need for a special kind of support during this vulnerable state after childbirth. This support depends on her relationship with the older women around her.

In history, older women were always the providers of postnatal knowledge and the givers of care. When 'the nannies' of Māori tradition care for the mother at this moment of life, they are not just putting her back together again: a deeper process of mothering is also being taught. It is as if, by having the role of mother modelled for her by her carer, she can come more fully into her own role as mother.

Each time a woman gives birth she is initiated and re-initiated into motherhood simply by being cared for, and the practical help that goes with this allows her to be rested and healthy too. Thus her capacity for mothering is strengthened.

It is well known that social support is one of the biggest determinants of public health in general.[1] This is especially true for the health of new mothers. A recent study from RMIT in Melbourne concluded there was more emotional distress reported after childbirth when parents had expected to be, and were, independent of wider support. On the other hand, those who expected, and received, family or social network support expressed the most positive emotional response to their postpartum. The group expecting to do it alone also reported feeling overwhelmed, ashamed, self-doubting, angry and anxious.[2]

Social support after birth may be even more important than the outcome of the birth:

> How she [the mother] gives birth really contributes to how easily and quickly she will fall in love with her baby, but it doesn't determine it. She can have an awful time in others' eyes and end up with a caesar [caesarean section] and a general anaesthetic, and still have fantastic support around her and believe she is really important as a mother. The whole culture of women's families, of them as a mother, is a big part of it. The value of women in the family... - *Carly Francis, midwife*

There is an important point here, which is that positive attitudes begin at the family level. When a family empowers itself to promote good values around motherhood and care of the mother, it provides the foundation for proper support and it sends a healthy message to all its members. This includes the children, who can then pass it on to future generations.

A vital part of this message is the honouring of the mother. She is honoured in appreciation of her bravery, for her role as 'the canoe which conveys one generation to the next' (a traditional Māori view) and for bringing those around her closer to the beauty and mystery of giving life. In the 1980s, anthropologists Gwen Stern and Laurence Kruckman proposed that there was a correlation between certain components of the social support women receive after giving birth, and improved mental health.[3] These included a structured period of rest in a secluded environment, mothering and protection of the mother, and giving practical help, which have already been discussed here. The other important component they included was the recognition of the mother's new status, or the honouring of the mother. To honour someone raises their status and lowers their stress response, and lowering the stress response normalizes cortisol levels and strengthens the nervous system and the immune system, as discussed in Chapter Two. Therefore this becomes an obvious strategy for healing and emotional transition. It is so obvious that the question can even be asked, why would you *not* do this after childbirth?

Her new status is also acknowledged verbally, in simple ways, such as addressing her as 'the new mother' for several months after the birth. In North Africa, there is a special greeting for a woman who has given birth to twins. She is regarded as blessed, *baraka* which means 'full of blessedness', and her hand is kissed and she is addressed as '*lalla*', 'my lady'.[4] There are also rituals of honouring. For example, in the Middle East, North Africa and South Asia, the new mother takes part in a henna ritual where her feet (especially) are covered with intricate patterns.[5] This is not only a celebration of her new status, but in order to preserve the beautiful designs she has to rest and is discouraged from getting up to do housework. (Henna is also used in this tradition to offer psychic protection when the mother is psychologically vulnerable after birth.) Throughout the world it is very common for the mother to receive gifts for herself, and not just for the baby (as is the common Western custom). In Mali women are given lengths of cloth with the words, 'to carry the baby in'. There are often gifts of special food delicacies. These practices of honouring exist in a great many traditions and they indicate to us that this is the mother's moment to be a heroine and the centre of attention. And it is not just for the first few days after the birth, but for the entire Golden Month that this happens. In Anjalika's case, it lasted even longer.

Anjalika (who described her warming massage in Chapter Three) was brought up in a village in Sri Lanka. Her story began with difficulties, but ended well. Anjalika was 22 years old and in love with a man whose parents considered her to be socially inferior. The same day that she realized her period was late, her fiancé was killed in a car accident. I touched my tummy and told him I thought I was pregnant, and then he died later that day in an accident. My family and my village wouldn't take me when the pregnancy was known and I went to stay with a friend, but then I got very bad dysentery and had to go to hospital and have IV fluids. The doctor wanted me to abort because he thought the baby had been injured by the dysentery and dehydration, and then my mother-in-law came to visit and wanted me to abort too because I was too young and on my own, but I said 'no' to them both and left the hospital.

Everyone says you must be happy during the pregnancy or the baby will be affected, but I just prayed and felt mentally strong and asked for a healthy baby. I felt a beautiful connection to my son and reassured him I would look after him. The next seven months I stayed at a Mother Theresa orphanage. They were kind and respectful there, but no one visited me. The orphanage was having to beg at the market for food, but just before I gave birth my mother-in-law finally came and she brought me a lot of good food. My mother visited only once. Finally my brother came and brought me home and then took me to hospital to have my baby. My father died within an hour of me giving birth, although I didn't know it at the time, and again no one came for five days because of the funeral.

Finally my mother-in-law came to see me. When she saw that my son had an identical birthmark in the same place on his body as his father, her son, she could finally admit that it was her son's baby. Now a beautiful chapter began in my life. I went to live with my in-laws and my mother-in-law cared for me so well I will never forget her. I was given daily massage, a specially prepared diet, and I did nothing at all for three months. My father-in-law carried my son everywhere with him, even up until he was five years old! - *Anjalika, Sri Lanka*

Eventually Anjalika left Sri Lanka and remarried, but because of the bonds created in this early time between her son, herself and her first in-laws, she remains very close to them. She says she will always be grateful that they gave her and her son the best beginning that she could wish for.

Another key element for support to be successful is that it is welcome: the mother's needs are respected and she is given her space. Mothers need a sense of control at this vulnerable time of transition when so many things are beyond their control: being told what to do and what not to do is not helpful. As Lucia, who tells her story in the next chapter, comments, not everyone wants to be confined inside an apartment for six weeks after giving birth. For some women, the idea may be unbearable. Hong Kong and Taiwanese studies[6, 7, 8] even suggest that confinement which is not perceived as helpful is a risk factor for developing postpartum depression. If support feels imposed in a way that the mother feels constrained, and she feels in conflict with the rituals of her tradition, then it is not useful support.

Organized and consistent support is the most helpful kind of support. It is not enough to honour and praise the new mother, she also needs practical care such as daily regular meals or a massage, delivered as she has planned and expects it. All levels of the support she receives need to be consistent.

When there is no strong cultural tradition to frame a woman's expectations of how she will be looked after, it will be useful for her to take time to plan with family and friends what support she will need after giving birth. This is not always straightforward. She may ask how she can know what she will need when there are so many variables, such as how the birth will be, how the baby will be. How can she have any idea of what she will need if she hasn't given birth before?

Some of these difficulties are illustrated in Carolina's story:

> Carolina was from Argentina and her partner from Germany. Neither had been long in New Zealand

before they fell in love, and Carolina soon became pregnant. Even though the pregnancy was unplanned, she was happy and healthy throughout her nine months and she assumed that after the birth things would continue in the same way. She and her partner had hoped for a water birth, but the labour turned out to be long and difficult and this was not possible. Her perineum tore badly during the birth, leading to an infection and many months of pain. It was difficult for her to move around, and having sex was unthinkable. Alone during the day while her partner worked, she became lost in relentless pain, fatigue and sleep deprivation. She says, 'I became just Maiya's mum, nothing else'.

Eventually she was saved by a local community group who insisted and even paid for her to get in a taxi and come to their centre for rest. There, she felt confident that her baby was well cared for, and she was able to get the sleep she needed. She was also very lucky to have a partner who supported her emotionally beyond what she imagined he could do, especially as they hadn't been together long.

In the end Carolina was able to return to Argentina for a few months when her daughter was six months old, but she is certain that she will not give birth again without being with her family and in her own culture. 'I have been brave once,' she said. 'That is enough. Back home you are never left alone after giving birth. There is always someone popping in to bring treats – your neighbours, your family, friends. In New Zealand I received a lot of flowers, but I was alone'.

Carolina had no idea what she would need after giving birth and she didn't know she would need support. Her isolation was worsened by the fact that she was a new immigrant without a community around her, and she could not communicate well in English. This resulted in her having to face her difficulties mostly alone.

The father

> 'The 40 days' is a moment when the woman's world is in the forefront: it is a time of support. The men are not very visible. The discussion is all about the woman and baby. But we try really hard behind the scenes. We are constantly alert to make sure that mum and baby are fine, and trying to make sure that any good thing can be provided for her. – *Boubacar, Malian father*

The father's/partner's support is crucial to the success of the Golden Month. Whether the partner is a man or woman, he (or she) is the one who provides the structure for the mother to be able to 'sit' in the Golden Month. The father/partner is also a go-between connecting the family with the world outside, and protecting the mother at this moment from having to deal with responsibilities other than herself and her new baby. At the same time he (or she) is tuning in to an intense internal experience of loving, together with the mother and baby. Men also release oxytocin when their baby is born (although not in such large quantities as women), just as other consistent carers of the new baby do. This helps them to become parents to that baby. Like mothers and babies, their brains change to become more trusting, calm and loving. A similar hormone to oxytocin, vasopressin, which helps form social bonds, is also released and men may find they rise to the occasion of fatherhood beyond their own expectations. But as with mothers, for oxytocin and vasopressin to be well established fathers must be also given the opportunity to come close to the source of the loving, to have unhurried space and close contact with the world of the newborn. So the father's/partner's role is complex and can involve some fine balancing between the inner and outer worlds.

If partners are able to take time off work, even for a short time, they can become fully involved in the slow rhythm of household life which revolves around care of the mother and baby. In the Mexican tradition, men step fully into the postnatal world during *la cuarentena*, the 40-day postnatal ritual which involves the extended family in caring for the mother and the newborn baby. While the mother is resting, the responsibility for household tasks are taken over by her partner, who either does them himself or, if he is working, is responsible for overseeing that they are done. The father gains confidence in care of the baby by learning from the mother, who in turn has received instruction from her mother or mother-in-law. This helps him centre on family life, get close to his child and feel confident in parenting.[9]

> I looked after each one of my girls after their deliveries. I was a bit of an ogre and wouldn't let just anyone visit but the girls used to say, 'That is great, mum, you are doing the right thing.' An unexpected benefit of being in their homes was that although I didn't set out with this an as objective, it really worked out that I got closer to my sons-in-law. Even one whom I didn't have much to do with before the birth got quite close to me and visits me by himself even now. – *Noelene, grandmother, New Zealand*

The Golden Month is an opportunity to strengthen all relationships in the family and the community around it. This happens through the common task of looking after the mother, and from being close to the special loving, oxytocin-laden state of mother and baby. Noelene was able to strengthen her relationship with her sons-in-law this way, by working with them to care for her daughters in their homes.

In this situation we acknowledge our dependence upon one another, our interdependence. In Western culture, independence is regarded as a virtue and something to aspire to in many areas of life. However if we struggle to become independent too early after childbirth, we risk isolating ourselves from help when we most need it, while our mothers, sisters and friends are waiting (sometimes desperately!) to be involved. Our isolation in turn can feed an illusion of separateness from those around us, which does not help us to flourish.

Being able to depend on others when in need is just as much a virtue as being independent. In the different cultures which follow some form of Golden Month, the mother is allowed to, and allows herself to, be fully dependent on others. When those she is relying on offer her care which she welcomes, not only does she receive their support, but her levels of happiness and pride are amplified through being reflected back to her by others. Her feelings of belonging are enhanced and stress levels drop. It does not matter (except for the elders!) that everyone helping the mother gets exhausted and sleep-deprived in serving her needs. Her helpers are not in the process of recovering from childbirth and they are not breastfeeding: they have more resilience to bounce back than she does. It is part of their investment in her future health and well-being. The mother, on the other hand, is taking her time to rest and rebuild her vitality. Later on, her own turn will come to look after her sisters, friends, daughters, nieces and granddaughters.

Interdependence, where there is a give and take of duties and rewards towards others in a group, is easy to achieve in cultures where an extended family or community operates well. In these cultures and sub-cultures each woman responds to the demands of the one whose turn it is to receive help, and at the same time she feels quite at ease when it is her own turn to ask for help. When I was talking with mothers from strong postpartum traditions, I was struck by how these women felt entitled to ask for proper care. It was refreshing to see no one was hanging back or being a martyr. And no one was accusing the mother of being selfish.

Letting go of independence can be a challenge, especially when we are brought up with the consistent message of how highly prized it is. Even though someone from outside of Western culture might not understand why a mother would insist on her independence at this time (in a life of hard work, why not ask for help when you can?), it also depends on those around you to give you permission to feel entitled. So this part is not always so easy to do for mothers in the West. However, as long as she remains in control of her decisions, and her needs are truly being served, it greatly benefits the mother to take the support that is offered, and enjoy being dependent on others for these short few weeks of her Golden Month.

***

1. Wilkinson and Pickett. *The Spirit Level*, p.277.

2. R. Kokanović, et al, (eds). Paths to Parenthood: Emotions on the Journey through Pregnancy, Childbirth, and Early Parenting (Palgrave Macmillan, 2018), pp.187-214.

3. G. Stern and L. Kruckman. 'Multi-Disciplinary Perspectives on Post-Partum Depression: An Anthropological Critique', *Social Science and Medicine*, 1983; (17).

4. C. Cartwright Jones. 'Traditional Postpartum Rituals of India, North Africa and the Middle East: Seclusion, Henna, & 40 day Homecare', *Born to Bloom: Resources for Women's Development, Aware Birth, and Beyond*, 2002, website: http://www.lotusfertility.com/Postpartum_Wisdom_Rituals.html.

5. Ibid.

6. S. Grigoriades, G. Erlick Robinson, K. Fung, et al. 'Traditional Postpartum Practices and Rituals: Clinical Implications', *La revue Canadienne de Psychiatrie*, 2009; 54(12): 834–40.

7. S. S. Heh, L. Coombes and H. Bartlett. 'The Association Between Depressive Symptoms and Social Support in Taiwanese During the Month', *International Journal of Nursing Studies*, 2004; 41(5): 573–9.

8. D. T. S. Lee. 'Postnatal Depression in Hong Kong Chinese'. PhD diss., Chinese University of Hong Kong, 2000. Dissertation Abstracts International, 61 (08-B), 4076.

9. K. Niska, M. Snyder and B. Lia-Hoagberg. 'Family Ritual Facilitates Adaptation to Parenthood', *Public Health Nursing*, Oct 1998; 15(5): 329–37.

Chapter Five

Stories from Mothers

The stories mothers from around the world told me about their post-birth experiences are an indispensable part of this book. It was a delight to be part of their discussions in homes, courtyards and offices, and all the women I spoke to were enthusiastic in sharing their experiences and in wishing for better care for mothers everywhere.

I am sharing here the interviews with six women from very different countries. They represent Asia, the Pacific, Africa, the Middle East, South America and Europe. The women talk about the mother's special status after childbirth, and her strengths, vulnerabilities and needs. They also relate the challenges and difficulties of the transition each birth brings. Some, like Kadjiatou and Ngangouma from Mali, and Puja from India, have been introduced already in previous chapters. The others make their first appearance below. I have tried to select a group of interviews which complement each other in presenting a range of experiences within the commonalities of their traditions. There were many more interviews I would have liked to include but couldn't because of space, but sometimes it has been possible to share the experiences of those women elsewhere in the book in shorter quotes.

Mali

I interviewed three women in Bamako, the capital of Mali and a city of about 2 million inhabitants. They are all Bambara, one of the largest ethnic groups in Mali, but as they pointed out, the traditions they describe are practiced by all ethnic groups throughout Mali, and all religions, Christian, Muslim and animist.

The three women were: Ngangouma, a retired farmer, mother of ten and grandmother of 52; Hawa, a mother of five; and Kadjiatou, a young mother with her two-month-old son, her second child. The interview took place in a courtyard in a suburb of Bamako. It was conducted in Bambara and translated for me by Ngangouma's son. This particular interview was also filmed. The cameraman and sound engineer were both fathers, and enthusiastically supported 'the 40 days' themselves.

Ngangouma: Jenny, I wish to talk to you about my child-bearing experience. I had ten children and never had any problems. My mother-in-law looked after me very well and whenever I gave birth she helped me. She would wash me and the baby with traditional herbs and massaged us with a mixture of shea butter and traditional herbs.[1] She usually massaged me daily as long as I needed it for the first 40 days. She would give me honey to cleanse my stomach[2] and fed me chicken soup, fresh fish soup, and eggs. She also gave me other meat and fruit. This diet allows the mother to regain her strength and re-establish herself.

With this complete care from my mother-in-law each time I gave birth, I gave birth ten times without any problems. For 40 days all I would do was feed my baby and lie next to him or her. She carried the baby and completely looked after him whenever he needed it. I did nothing, no work at all, not even domestic work. She was a very good and caring woman – she always said that as she did not give birth to a daughter herself, I was her first daughter.

My children never gave me problems. They usually did not cry. So right from the beginning they gave me no problems and then they looked after me when they grew up. I wish the same thing for you – that your children look after you in your old age.

I am a member of the group of elderly women who advise the Western medical midwife after each birth in the village. We advise the family on how to care for the mother and baby. We always ask the mother to have her 40 days' rest and be cared for by the rest of the family. The mother of the newborn is always treated like a queen. She is well fed and does no work until after 40 days. It is important to remember that honey and chicken soup are very important for her. At the end of 40 days the woman has become strong and her body is well relaxed. If she does 'the 40 days', with God's will she will subsequently have fewer health problems. I will let the others talk now.

Hawa: I am Hawa Doumbia. I have five children and did not have any problems with any of them. With each birth I adopted 'the 40 days'. I always drank warm water too. In our culture warm water makes it easier to cleanse your lower abdomen after childbirth. Cold water makes the blood [the vaginal discharge after birth] stagnate and it does not come out easily. I also boiled bamboo leaves, drank some as tea and washed myself with the rest. I was massaged too. These things give you strength. I will now let Kadjiatou talk.

Kadjiatou: I am Kadjiatou Coulibaly and I wish to talk about my experience after giving birth. Once I left the hospital my sister-in-law looked after me totally. She fed me correctly and allowed me the 40 days' rest. She has been massaging me daily (with this baby). All I do is eat and sleep. I have not had any difficulties because of her care... She washes the baby and lays him next to me. All I have to do is give him breastmilk, eat and sleep. My baby is two months old now and I still don't do any work (neither household duties nor paid employment)...

In the past we, the Bambara people, used to consider 'the 40 days' also as a way of having space between the man and wife. Tradition allowed us to stay with an elderly woman so that the husband didn't ask for sexual relations with us. To me that is not the important point of 'the 40 days'. The main point is that after birth the woman is as weak as a chicken. You can easily fall if someone just touches you. You cannot endure any mental or physical strain. Being well fed and rested for 40 days allows you to recover mentally and physically. After that you can go about the routine things of your life without difficulty. So 'the 40 days' is not to avoid sexual relations but to re-establish yourself. Afterwards you can restart your marriage on a good footing. If you don't take the rest you are very tired. People cannot tell what is wrong but you are mentally and physically exhausted. The baby will always be crying too - you are trying your best but you can be very sick inside without anyone noticing... If you see me like this it is because of the 40 days' rest. That is why I am feeling very good in myself. I feel so good in myself and so healthy that I could run and climb that tree.

Jenny: What role do the men play in 'the 40 days'?

Hawa: Men have an important role in 'the 40 days' too.

Ngangouma: They are the ones who have to pay for all the food – so the men's help is crucial in the process. Without them none of these things can be done. If the woman who has given birth has to run around like everyone else, working to get food, that is not good for her.

Hawa: When a woman becomes sick after birth because of lack of rest, it is a very harsh experience... It can also cost a lot of money when you get complications after the birth. In the offices here in Mali, women have three months paid maternity leave. This is obligatory in all private companies here too.

Ngangouma: For the Bambara people 'the 40 days' is an obligation. It is adopted regardless of the amount of work to be done, or whether it is the rainy or dry season. When you recover then you can start work.

The actual birth is not the end of the process. Afterwards, your body is open and vulnerable. They say in our culture that when you give birth, the 'tomb is open'. It is only after 40 days that the angels close the tomb.

Please tell your women that they should rest for 40 days, stop work and look after themselves. There will still be money to be made when you return to work... If you rush back (to work) you may end up spending all of your savings, and more, on medicines, and then in the end you lose even more time. Jenny, if you tell them that and they listen, it would be great. But no matter what you say, some people still may not listen. However, you will have done your duty.

India

Puja is originally from India and her husband is Italian. She is in her late 20s and works as a counsellor. She gave birth in New Zealand to her first child, three-month-old Sawyl. Prior to coming to New Zealand she had lived in Italy for 10–15 years.

Her mother and father were both present at this interview. They had come from India for several months to help look after Puja and her baby boy, and were keen to take part in the discussion about their Indian tradition of postnatal care.

Jenny: How was the birth of your baby?

Puja: Overall it was very good. This was my first baby and I have been here in New Zealand for the last four years and after two years we decided we were ready to have a baby because we really like the country and the overall health system. I enjoyed the service at the hospital and the system that lets you choose your own midwife. [This is a free nationwide service.] It doesn't exist anywhere else in the world that I know of.

I was born in India where we don't have that extra special care. Even in Italy this doesn't exist either. So we were really excited that we would have it, and it turned out to be fantastic. Seeing the midwife every month before the birth and then the service at the hospital was amazing. We were really happy with the services of the other midwives, and the doctors also. I wouldn't change anything.

Jenny: How were you cared for after the birth?

Puja: I went to Birthcare [a maternity hospital] afterwards.

So it was fantastic – three days of not worrying about anything, and in the middle of the night the midwife would come and look after Sawyl and see I was feeding right. Because it was all new, I didn't know anything, and so I was anxious and overwhelmed, and also tired and exhausted. It was great having proper meals on time, great meals, just what I needed after birth. I hardly slept the first three nights, but during the day I would drift off in the afternoon.

It was also a fantastic feeling coming home after three days. I had my husband here when Sawyl was born, then my mother-in-law came from Italy after a few weeks and now my parents have arrived just three weeks ago.

Also, the first day I came home, one of my friends arrived from India for two weeks, so the timing was great. My friend understood the kind of needs I had because she is Indian too. Proper meals. Massage. She gave me massage every day. I would have some rest. She would take Sawyl with her for a walk and she would come and just say to me, 'Take an hour off,' and I would have some rest. I have a fantastic husband too – he is very supportive – so he had some days off work, even though he didn't get parental leave. I didn't have to worry about cleaning or cooking or anything.

As for her giving me massage, in India we all know massage from childhood because we have massage as children from our parents or from an aunt, and we would also have a special person coming home to give us massage from day one of our lives. So we sort of learn automatically that this is how you receive massage, this is how you give it. For example, if I was having a pain in my back or shoulders she would concentrate on that particular area. Also I had just given birth so it was a special massage, not just one that is given to everyone.

Jenny: Did she massage your abdomen?

Puja: Yes, she did. Then after she left I asked a professional lady to come in. She is an Indian massage therapist and she gave me massage on my tummy [abdomen] for a week, because I needed something for my tummy as well. It needed energy. I found it was just empty-feeling. Everything had been taken out.

She had different oils. She asked what I would like and I chose sweet almond oil... She would also advise me to keep warm, especially around the lower back and tummy. She would say, 'Don't get cold or you will start getting some really bad aches and pains in your back.' I replied to her that I was used to this country and the weather, but later I realized that I needed some special extra care for my lower body. So I was keeping some hot wheat bags and hot water bottles there, and even just a pashmina shawl tied around my hips, which we use at home in India in winter. After the massage I would tie it there and keep the area really warm because that is what you really need after a massage too, not going into a cold place or getting cold air on your tummy.

Massage really helped me to recover from the weakness after the birth.

Jenny: Are there any special rules for resting after birth in Indian culture?

Puja: I was told to rest whenever I felt like it, because your body tells you when to stop. Personally I am an active person and during the day it didn't make sense to me to go to bed or rest, only at night-time to sleep. I worked until week 35 [of the pregnancy] because I wanted to be active and use my muscles and I didn't want to sit at home and do nothing. So I was doing yoga. After the birth I was advised to continue with yoga every day, but not immediately, just when I felt I was ready and could feel that it would be beneficial. As for resting, I learned that I had to stop and go to myself, 'Okay, you have a nap now.'

The first six weeks they say you need to be careful and not do anything heavy, and I did listen. My husband did all the house chores. Even now that Sawyl is 14 weeks old, I am still careful.

Jenny: What about diet after birth?

Puja: I had a lot of support. Before my friend came from India I had another friend, also Indian, who lives here in New Zealand. At Birthcare she brought me milk full of almonds, and chapattis with ghee, and she said, 'You have just given birth and you need to eat this as well,' even though I was also getting the meals at Birthcare. That was fantastic! So my health was okay.

When I came home from Birthcare, my friend from India was cooking for me. I was talking to my mother on the phone from India and she would ask if we were eating ghee once a day. There is a special sweet dish made from ghee and flour and lots of dried fruits and almonds that is eaten just after we give birth for the first 40 days. It is called *panjeeri*. The first 40 days are considered really important. We are careful what we are eating. We don't even go near the kitchen for the first 40 days. I didn't do any cooking at all. I had my friend and then my mother-in-law, and she cooked all the traditional Italian meals for me so that I would have good lactation. So, I had Indian food for the first two weeks and then Italian food. I had a lot of meat and pasta – they say that 'carbs' are really good. And then my mother-in-law would cook some special dishes I had never eaten before, especially for mothers. They had parmesan and eggs and flour in them.

Puja's mother: In India the mother is also given milk three times a day and almonds for the calcium, and green cardamom.

Puja's father: And *khichari* (rice soup) with ghee also because it is really soft and not heavy food.

Puja's mother: And lentils with rice, *mung dhal*. When I gave birth myself I had very good care. My mother-in-law wouldn't let me in the kitchen for 40 days. She gave me those same foods that I talked about, and she also took the baby for me and gave me massage. There was a lady who specialized in massage coming to our home every day as well, for 40 days.

Jenny: What is the role of the father after the birth?

Puja's father: The husband's role is important in India. When my wife gave birth I would help out in the evening after work by going to the market. In the Indian tradition the first 40 days are very important, then after 40 days it is not like, after 40 days, here you go and all your responsibilities are back. Gradually you get back to your routine. For a woman to become a mother, you know, it is a big job. If my wife was tired I could go in the kitchen myself. Also we used to live in the joint family: my father had five brothers, my mother had five sisters. They would exchange their experiences and aunties would come and help.

Puja: Men's role is to give emotional support as well as practical support. That is what you can get from your husband. In India there is no system that allows the husband to be present at the birth, as he can be here or even in Italy. This system (in New Zealand) makes it possible to have your partner at the birth, which gives emotional comfort. I imagine that not having the husband present at the birth could create nervousness, anxiety. But the kind of support that Indian men can provide after the birth is very important too.

Jenny: Are all these practices still done after the birth in India?

Puja's mother: They are compulsory in the Indian family. The values around it are so strong...

Puja: India is different now. It is very modern but we still continue to have our cultural values and our system, as my mother said. It is compulsory. You've got to do it! You cannot change.

If you don't look after yourselves in the first few months just after the birth with good diet, massage and sleep, you are going to feel it anyway. You must (look after yourself) or you will start to feel weak. That is when it might be too late to work on, because then you might have to go to the doctor and say, 'My backache is really bad now,' or, 'I am not able to sleep because I am overtired.' You might get into postnatal depression because overtiredness can do this, also if you don't have the support with you. So looking after yourself after the birth is really, really important.

Romania

Lucia has two young sons, and is married to a New Zealand

Māori . Her family lives in Romania. Lucia's experience as an immigrant mother in a cross-cultural marriage reflects the difficulties of an unsupported postpartum, away from familiar healthcare routines and traditions. She works as an ethnic affairs advisor and is currently studying for a PhD.

Jenny: What was your experience after you gave birth to your children?

Lucia: The first shock after I gave birth to my first child was that in a couple of hours I had to get dressed, get baby dressed, hop in the car and drive to Birthcare.[4] I was shocked because I didn't expect to have to get out of bed. At Birthcare it was the weekend and they had only one staff member for ten women, so even though they were wonderful staff they weren't able to assist us with information and everything and many of us were new mothers and the midwife wasn't present at all... I do realize now that it was my responsibility that I didn't make a better relationship with the midwife. I was thinking, 'It is her duty because she is paid to do that,' and she obviously didn't think so.

I was exhausted after three days of labour and the baby in the next bed was screaming all night. The mother was a teenage mother, very nice, but she also didn't know much – at one stage I saw her falling asleep in the sitting room with her baby because she was being considerate and didn't want to bother me. The next night my baby screamed all night because my milk hadn't come in and I realized that is what babies do, but no one was there to tell us or support us at that moment. They gave us information sheets but I needed practical help and when I asked for help they said, 'Where is your husband, where is your family?' I don't have any family here and in Romania the hospital stay is four to five days and the men are not allowed to visit even. They keep apart from this 'women's business'. Back then I used to think it was not his job, so I felt very uncomfortable about having my husband there, having to rely so much on him. I wasn't ready for the New Zealand system and I thought they were paid to take care of you and therefore they should take care of you.

With my second baby my expectations were really low. After two nights in the hospital they kicked me out. I was begging them to let me stay another night so I could get more rest but they explained that it wasn't possible – the hospital was full and there was no place for us. I rode home on a rainy cold evening, already dark, and my mother-in-law had cooked us dinner which we appreciated very much, and then she left. I was more confident this time, but there were some very tough moments. When Alex was one week old I had to take Mihai [Lucia's first son] to A&E because he was sick and I had to carry him. I was thinking, 'My gosh, it is only a week since I gave birth, is this alright?'

In the process of establishing breastfeeding there is a terrible moment (I knew about it in Romania). If you get cold, then you feel like electricity is going through your breasts and whole body. It is just for a short time but you feel panicky and stuck. It happened with Mihai and then Alex. With Alex it was the middle of the night and I was trying to cover myself and get warm and Alex started to cry in his cot. Luckily I had my cell phone. I phoned my husband who was asleep in the other room with Mihai. He moaned but he brought me a cup of hot soup and a sandwich. I was already thinking I would bring the microwave into the bedroom and move into the bedroom.

They were tough moments when I would have appreciated more help. My family wasn't there. Mind you, they offered to come but I insisted they come later when I had to return to work in three months. My husband is from a large and supportive Māori family, all of them brothers, but it was hard for me to ask for help. I didn't know what I could ask for. For the first baby they visited daily and would bring food, which was really nice, like Romania, because in Romania female relatives bring food, tidy the house and help with the baby. They brought takeaways, though, which was not what I needed. One week after Mihai was born I jumped in the car and went to the supermarket for vegetables and things for soup. I am sure that whatever I asked for they would have done, but I realized that for me there was a difference between blood family and adoptive family, because I just couldn't ask them. So I suffered from a lack of support and cultural understanding, and a lack of a set of traditions that would keep me and my baby 'safe'. Probably with more support I would have been a better parent. Certainly I would have been a better companion!

Jenny: What happens after birth in Romania?

Lucia: In Romania the hospital stay is four to five days. Not so long ago the mother and child were separated from each other in the belief that the mother needed the rest. The child was brought for breastfeeding and then taken away. Hospitals were closed and no one was allowed to visit. They tried to be infection-proof and didn't even accept flowers and the mother would have to wave to the relatives from the window. Before this, in the traditional village model, the mother would not leave the premises for six weeks. It was a way to protect the mother because the physical work in the village would be quite hard and this would give her time inside with her baby. Female relatives traditionally come over bringing food, and they clean and tidy so that the mother can relax. They still do that, although mothers needed more physical support in traditional times, because there were no washing machines, etc. Last time I went to Romania, my mother and I went to visit a relative with wine and chocolate! However the idea was still there to bring food. This goes on for six weeks. Of course now there are a lot of options but there are still families that respect this tradition very much. My cousin who gave birth recently had her mother and mother-in-law coming daily for six weeks to do all these things for her. I remember feeling jealous, but when she told me that she didn't go out of her little apartment for six weeks I didn't know whether I would choose the freedom to do what I wanted or be looked after like this!

There is another idea which is important in Romania and it is that the baby has godparents who are really important in the family structure. A couple is given two sets of godparents, for both the husband and the wife, and they bring a lot of support after birth, a kind of Māori *whakawhanaunga tanga*. They oversee the well-being of the family. It doesn't work in practice for my family here as we are far away, but they can still offer a model of how to be a good family. They are the spiritual parents of the baby: normally they baptize the baby and bring material and emotional support. In our tradition the godmother has a very important role in bringing food and advice after the birth.

Jenny: Is there any special advice for the mother?

Lucia: As I said, the food is brought to the mother: she is not allowed to cook. Chicken soup is considered very healthy and beer is given to help breastfeeding. I did ask for beer when I was in the hospital and it helped, at least it relaxed me. We do place importance on keeping warm and keeping out of draughts. You can't stay ina room with the windows and doors open as the draught will make you and the baby sick. The windows are opened for five to ten minutes to keep the air fresh, preferably with mum out of the room. A towel is also put around the waist to keep this area of the body warm and to help support the abdomen and muscles as they recover.

In my tradition, the first six weeks are important for a mother to rest, but it is not as if she is doing nothing. At that time she has more important things to do: these are to bond with her baby and adjust to her new life, and to make a basis for a healthy family life. So actually, it is very important and hard work when you think of establishing breastfeeding and putting new things into your routine. The Romanian government offers all mothers one full year of paid maternity leave and the women in the family provide the support needed. There is free healthcare, although you still need to tip the health professionals.

Over one third of Aucklanders are immigrants [40% according to a study in 2011],[5] so we have a big need here to increase our awareness of migrant mothers' experiences and needs. This will inform best practice in their care. I think mothers, and especially new mothers, should have a choice about what kind of care they receive after birth and what level of support. While New Zealand offers great services, they concentrate on providing information and advice, which rather puts pressure on a new migrant mother, I found, when what I really needed was good food, plenty of rest and help with the house chores. Certainly they should be allowed to stay longer in hospital if they think they need to. Encouraging families and community to step in is nice, but not so relevant for new migrant mothers who don't have that network.

Samoa

This interview took place at the West Auckland Pacific Island Health Centre, Fono, where Galuafi Lui was working as a breastfeeding consultant at the time. She is now Pacific Island Liaison Coordinator at the Waitemata Health Maternity Unit. She is the mother of four girls and one son.

Jenny: Can you tell me about your Samoan tradition of caring for the mother?

Galuafi: My experience with the Samoan tradition is through seeing my own mother and her four sisters giving birth. Most of these were homebirths where the extended family knew when the labour started.

During the labour the father, and sometimes other men, will prepare a *vaisalo* (a nourishing meal made from young coconut) for the *failele* (new mum).

After birth the mother will be resting. The first week is very special. The grandmother or an elderly aunt will sleep with the mother and baby, but not the husband. These special ladies will help the new baby burp after breastfeeding and then allow mum to rest. This is the time grandmother will provide advice to the new mum on how to look after herself and her health, and regain her strength. Other family members care for her too by providing food, doing the washing, housework and other women's duties. The husband will also help provide what is needed, as well as looking after the other children.

'It takes a village to raise a child' - this is literally true in our culture. The extended family all help to raise this baby. It is very special that baby will be born in an open *fale* (home).

In traditional Samoa the homes are open. The mats are put around the bath tub to protect baby from the wind and elements while grandmother sits in the middle, bathing the baby in warm water. Grandmother will then dress the baby and pass it to mum for feeding or putting to sleep.

Jenny: Is there a set period of rest?

Galuafi: It depends. Some new mothers may take longer to heal and recover. Mothers who have had several children may take less time to recuperate. It varies from a week to several weeks. During this time families will be there to wash the nappies, cook breakfast, lunch and dinner, bath the baby and generally take over and assist the mother in her usual duties while she recovers. Sometimes the grandmother offers a nice massage for the mother and then encourages her to stand up and wash herself. This process allows the mother to slowly start picking up her duties as she transitions to being totally independent and the family slowly withdraws from their tasks. For my mother it was about ten days when she would slowly start to sweep the floor, wash the dishes, very slowly return to her normal routine. But she didn't cook. My father was the only income earner in the house so he was working, but we had older nieces and nephews and they were in the kitchen doing the cooking. They always asked Mum, 'What would you like to eat today?' She had very special food for a few weeks. How long the mother is in her postnatal period depends on the family and how well the mother was coping. As soon as they see that she is coping well they start to withdraw, but they don't withdraw totally away from her: they will always be in contact with her, checking, 'Are you alright? Is there anything you want us to do?' So family support is there always. That is the biggest thing in our Samoan tradition.

Jenny: Is there any special food that the mother is given after giving birth?

Galuafi: Yes, after she has given birth, the first morning a vegetable or chicken soup will be ready for her. Something nice and warm. In the morning she has some traditional breakfast like vaisalo which is made from baby coconuts. The coconut is very soft inside. They boil this and it is really nice for mum. It is easy to digest like a porridge, and very nourishing, it is 'Samoan seven-up', no preservatives or anything, just clean from the tree! The other breakfast mum will eat is *supoesi*. This is made from the pawpaw. When the pawpaw is nice and ripe the flesh is extracted and boiled in water until it is soft. Then you add a little bit of sago and it is sweet in itself, you don't need sugar. And that gives mum energy and helps a lot with producing milk. My grandmother would also encourage my mother, 'Come on, eat, eat a lot of food.' That was one of my grandmother's jobs, because my mother sometimes wouldn't feel like eating. 'Come on sit up and eat, it will be good for you to produce more milk for baby.'

And at lunchtime the mum will have a piece of taro and chicken soup, always chicken soup or fish soup. The mums eat a lot of warm soup and vegetables. And drinking from the coconut is really good for baby.

My grandmother would say that because baby was inside the stomach, making it very warm, that you wouldn't want to upset the stomach when baby comes out and leaves that area cold. So you need to have something nice and warm to soothe where baby was. It makes a lot sense.

This special diet goes on for a couple of weeks. The first five days are crucial for the whole family, keeping all that support going.

The other thing was on the first night, after mum is all nice and clean – I saw my grandmother do this for my mother – she brings a lavalava and wraps it tightly around the waist and hips, covering the uterus, like a corset. This brings everything together and brings the 'bad' blood out. I did this for my girls as well. And I find that my mother doesn't have a dropping stomach because of this. She also said if you were able to lie on your stomach, to put a soft pillow under your uterus. This is like a self-massage to help the blood out. I saw my grandmother massage my mum too until she was comfortable and fine.

Jenny: How about social support after birth in Samoa?

Galuafi: There is not much postnatal depression in Samoa because you have your whole family there. In Samoa we like to stay together. If a woman in the family is pregnant everyone is so looking forward to that baby. Everyone loves it. But when you come here to New Zealand, you live in your own small house, usually with a fence around it, and don't have contact with anyone. And if you don't have family, who would you turn to? So the mother can go into depression. In our tradition there is a lot of support. And everyone in the family witnesses the growing up of this baby. If the baby hiccups, everyone will know about it! Or they might say to a child, 'Eh, you were the one who came out and you were screaming hard-out!' Everyone talks about those kinds of things and witnesses the growing up of this child.

Jenny: What was your personal experience being looked after?

Galuafi: I gave birth here [in New Zealand]. My own experience of being cared for was that I felt so relieved. It felt really good knowing that I had good support. My mother was there. My parents moved to New Zealand in 1982 with all my siblings. It strengthened me even before I had the baby, knowing that my family was there, my husband and my mother, and all my brothers and sisters waiting.

It strengthens you and you can't wait for this baby to come out and to take it home. It is just a great feeling. Even in Auckland I am so grateful to know that I know where all my family is. I know how to access their services, to turn to them if I need this or that. So having that knowledge and support from everyone you are close to is very, very important. It helps your mind. Your mind is so clear and happy and you are not stressed about anything so your breastmilk will just flow. There will be heaps of it.

There are a lot of visitors coming to you, a lot of family. That is what I love about our tradition: the support of the family and those who have loved you so much.

I have five children: four girls and one boy. When I had my first one here, my husband was overseas. He arrived on the day she was born, but he had to go back to the Islands because he was working there at the time. It was sad in a way because I really needed my husband, but he had to leave to go back and I understood that. But I was very happy to have my family with me: Mum (my expert), my sisters, my dad and brothers too. All their kind words and encouragement made me feel strong.

All of my children were born here. After my second child, we moved away from where Mum and Dad were, but they still came over and I had the support. I wanted to see them every day. It was something I had to do. My parents liked to count their grandchildren too. When I had my children I was a full-time mum. My mother had taught me well how to be independent and look after my own children. Even though I had the support of the family they have their own families to look after too. It is not as in Samoa where you all live in the same house and all do things together. Over here we had different houses to move to, but because you have that knowledge that you have seen and witnessed from your mother, you always carry it with you.

After I had my babies I wouldn't travel – my parents would come over and visit me every day of the week. I would start visiting my parents when my babies were about three or four months old. I would call and tell Mum, 'Don't come, we'll come to you now.' I remember Mum and Dad would always ask what I would like them to bring, keeping that tradition. I would try and tell them I had everything, but they would still bring something they knew I liked, my favourite food, or a pair of warm shoes.

Jenny: Can most Samoan families keep this support going here?

Galuafi: No, I don't think so, not many families here have that support. Some don't have their parents here. People come here on their own, and find their husband and have their babies here. It is very different how a lot of people have raised their children here. The other problem is financial. People feel they need to work: if you don't, you won't eat, won't survive. But then the relationship between mother and baby is neglected. I see a lot of mothers who are back to work three months after the baby is born. It is sad to see we are not looking after the generation of tomorrow. We are more worried about money. But I can understand where families are on this, because they need the money in order to live in this country, to pay the bills.

Through groups like our Titifaitama Breastfeeding Support Group, I can give support to the mothers. I used to have a lot of young mothers attending. Some didn't have husbands. I would try and get them together in order for them to get support and learn from each other. We try to create a safe atmosphere for them to share and discuss issues with each other, and since we are all going through the same thing, they start to open up with their problems. There was a young mother who had had a baby at a young age and the family didn't want her, so there was no support for her. She had brought embarrassment to her family (because she was unmarried). We went to her family and helped explain things. A lot of our people get embarrassed about this, it is the pride they have, to do with their names, the church. So the young ones get neglected with their new babies. Some young girls come from broken homes and you can never fix that – it becomes like a cycle. You can just do as much as you can, and they love coming to the group which becomes a refuge and a 'home' for them to receive support and reassurance. Another young woman came and just sat there, not saying anything. I told her just to say her name in Samoan and her baby's. I talked to her one-on-one to try to understand the issues and the things that were bothering her. She said she didn't like being around Samoans because of confidentiality issues and it all going back to the family. I try and acknowledge these women and praise them, show them that they mean something and that they are daughters of God. We instil in the women the idea of looking after themselves, and we provide tips for them on how to relieve stress. We encourage them to breastfeed and enjoy having their baby, because it is best for baby and financially better for the family. Another thing is that breastfeeding relaxes you and takes your mind off other things. It is a special opportunity to bond with and enjoy your baby.

We also discuss diet and nutrition as very important. We demonstrate what the healthy foods are by having healthy refreshments and snacks.

We discuss the importance of rest, especially the first few days after birth. I see a difference now when many mothers go into hospital, have the baby, then some are discharged on the same day back home and start cooking. It is a worry. They have no support and so they do not get enough time to recover their full strength.

Back in Samoa, birth is a very special time for the family and I am sure this is still the same back in the villages. I pray the tradition will continue. On that first night the whole family comes together and the minister says prayers to welcome the baby and there is a special meal. Nowadays, here in New Zealand, you go to hospital, come home and it is just you and your husband, and back to the normal routine.

The result is a lot of our babies now are not well looked after because the mothers don't have the support and knowledge. We need our mothers to be looked after properly, and we need for those young mothers to learn about our traditions and where they have come from, because our traditions and way of life we can learn from, and adapt some of these practices to help us raise a generation that is strong, and healthier than we were.

Druze

The Druze are an ethno-religious group living mostly in Northern Israel, Lebanon and Syria. They are a strong community that has kept its postpartum tradition alive for many generations, and the practices are typical of Middle Eastern postpartum practices in many respects. The Druze tradition particularly includes an awareness of the spiritual as well as physical and psychological processes of pregnancy and the postpartum.

This interview took place in a Druze town in the hills near Haifa, Israel, where we enjoyed wonderful hospitality in the home of Daliya. This included a cup of typical Druze post-partum tea with warm walnuts floating in it, a tea that has different variations around the Middle East but always features cinnamon and other warming herbs. Daliya is an acupuncturist dedicated to the health of her community, and an enthusiastic supporter of the Druze version of the Golden Month. Vardi translated the interview to and from Hebrew.

Daliya: The Druze tradition around the 40 days is very organised, agreed upon and caring, prescribed. This makes life so much easier, as you don't always need to think or worry about what to have or what to do. Everybody knows what is to be done.

The Druze see procreation as part of their religious practice, but the difference with Druze (and others) is that they are committed to quality of offspring, rather than quantity. Before conception we ensure that both the woman and man are healthy and strong.

In the first trimester it is very important that the woman rests a lot, avoids stimulating foods like meat and spices, and that she and those around her work together to keep her feeling calm. She eats sour foods like pickles, because sour astringes, draws together, and helps hold the pregnancy. After the first trimester she can eat plenty of grains and meat.

During pregnancy, all food is taken with awareness. There is a lot of emphasis on the quality of food: where we buy it and who the supplier is. If a place is selling cigarettes and alcohol - just selling it - we don't buy food from there. All meat, for example, must be halal. The person selling the meat is supposed to grow the meat, so you know what the animal ate before it was killed. You don't just go to the supermarket and buy meat and use it. You know exactly who grew the cow and how it was treated - that is if you want a really pure soul for the baby. [You eat] less industrial, processed food, and the grains, fruit and vegetables are from around where you live. So the provenance of all the food is known and [there is] no processed food, all natural is eaten.

Before birth the woman compiles for herself her list of wishes for herself and others. During the labour the mother is absolutely open.

Jenny: In the Māori and also the Malian tradition they say 'the mother is walking between worlds' at this time of the birth and the postpartum.

Daliya: Yes... she is between worlds, and so this is a very potent time spiritually where the intentions of wish and prayer are strong. She takes this list of wishes with her into labour.

So, after the birth, firstly, on a physical level ... Breakfast during the 40 days is warm milk, almonds, nuts, dates, meat and potatoes, labneh, za'atar, lots of garlic and eggs. The new mother doesn't prepare any of this, of course. She is not allowed in the kitchen or even to smell any cooking smells.

Breakfast is always taken very warm. Why is this? It is to make the blood move, to take out all the remains of blood that haven't come out, to shorten the period of bleeding and renew the blood. So this will help the mother to get up faster and have the power and energy to take care of her baby, and [this way] the bleeding is very short, because some women can have bleeding for more than a month. This special drink is taken in the morning:

1 litre *water*

1/3 cup *cinnamon sticks*

2–3 *pods cardamom*

1 *clove*

½ tsp *anise*

2 *English peppercorns*

2 slices *ginger* and a little *dry ginger*

A few pieces of *kulanjan (Alpinia galanga)*, which is anti-microbial, warm and promotes circulation of blood

You boil these ingredients together. Then some people add walnuts and maybe some pine nuts so that they warm in the drink. You usually put some sugar in the tea, otherwise it is a little bitter. You can make it less spicy if you want. You take it [the drink] in the morning, every day. It is also taken warm because losing the blood can make the body cold, so the new mother is more prone to 'wind and cold' [Chinese term], more vulnerable. Walnuts are nourishing the blood and influencing the brain so the mother will be calmer.

It is recommended that the mother doesn't leave the house for 40 days, not even outside the door, especially in wintertime, even not coming close to the windows: she is very vulnerable, and like you said earlier, she is also between worlds in those 40 days. So many bad things can happen, so she is well kept, well looked after.

Also [it is advised] not to take the baby out for 40 days because the Druze believe that the soul of the baby is descending down to him or her during those 40 days, and [it is] even important to keep him in a quiet, dark room so he can take his time and the soul can descend calmly... so don't take the baby out. So it takes 40 days for the soul of the baby to separate from his old family, from his previous life, and to reconnect with the new family and the new life.

So, the best thing for the baby is to see as few people as possible [at this time], for others not to kiss her, not to talk to her too much - only the mother and the father, because sometimes you see newborns smile suddenly, it is the baby reconnecting with the old life, so you don't want to interfere. You want the soul of the baby to be as clear and as pure as possible and not to get any influences. You know people are coming and saying, 'I want to hold him, he looks like this or that,' and doing all kind of 'show-offs' to everybody... No! No one is coming near the baby, and he is kept very quiet in a darkened room, only nursing and having his mother and father.

So, that was the physical [aspect of the practice]. Emotionally, the mother is very vulnerable too, so (she is) kept away from the news, from bad talking like gossip, from stressful events that are occurring around her, both personal and non-personal. Of course if there is something critical that she has to know then let her know, but otherwise she is very enclosed. Whatever you can spare her from, like, she doesn't have to know, it is not very important, just spare her. So, if there is some stressful event, or the mother, for example, fell and broke her arm, got some physical pain (during the 40 days), the physical pain can be treated and released completely only after another birth and another postpartum - a 'mending' experience.

If the postpartum was not good then the mother quite soon after tries to plan another pregnancy and to correct what happened before. [This idea is similar in Chinese medicine.]

Five Element theory [Chinese medicine] is also very much connected to the Druze tradition. So, this postpartum time, if there is some sort of stress, the mother is really encouraged to talk, to let it all out, to her partner, to her friends, to her sister, just talk and let it out. They call this 'nafas', which is like 'exhaling'. So you bring out everything, you exhale your emotions, your stagnating thoughts, and you become empty in order to renew yourself.

Another physical thing is that the mother is not doing anything. She is not allowed to do anything. She is not cleaning the house. Everybody is cleaning, cooking. She is not even allowed to squeeze a washcloth because it can make her joints painful, so she is like a queen.

So, all of this is keeping the woman very clear, pure, very strong, and the breast milk will also be very nourishing and high quality. It is the custom to breastfeed for two years, so if the 40 days are very good, she [the mother] is getting stronger and is well nourished, then the milk will be good for the whole two years. So this is really smart.

My own experience was that my father died suddenly and prematurely three months before I conceived my son. During my pregnancy I was sad, but I lived a very internally focused pregnancy and just stayed at home, worked in clinic and saw my family. I had a lot of support and also did psychotherapy and acupuncture. And so, even though I was sad, I felt very connected to my pregnancy and myself. I felt that although it was not an easy pregnancy, and I had a caesarean section after a long labour, the postpartum and my son himself made it a very special time, and now I think he is a very special and very strong child.

Jenny: You used the 40 days as a healing time in other ways too.

Daliya: Of course. My father was reincarnated in my sister's child. Kiran is her son. Aurian, my second son, had a hernia as a small baby and went into surgery and got neurological damage badly from the surgery, so he has some serious developmental deficiencies. They are all really supporting him. So, this is my nephew [shows photo], and we believe he is the reincarnation of my father. He has spoken and said, 'I am your father.' He told me, and my sister. Now he is six, but he told how as our father he helped build this house with my husband.

Vardi: What do you say to your father who is now your nephew?

Daliya: You hug him and you love him. He is telling a lot of details that there is no way he could have known, about his father, that is, the boy's great-grandfather. We didn't ask him anything – he was just telling us.

Vardi: In the community everyone is being reincarnated, so how come not everyone is telling things about their previous life?

Daliya: This is why the 40 days are very important, because if you keep the child very quiet, no TV, no music, not seeing many people, then the child is very clear and he can remember his previous life and bring this information to the present life. But if there was trauma, if someone was killed in a car accident or in a violent situation, Syria, the army, whatever, then the next life will be quite violent, and then those children come to me, to my clinic, to get treatment – re-establishing the previous life and making peace… mending this connection.

But if you don't give the newborn child quiet time, then he can't project and he won't hear those stories. So the 40 days is a really critical time so that the mother and the child can grow physically, spiritually and emotionally.

This is really science, because I see the women [in my clinic] before they get pregnant and during the pregnancy, and then after they give birth they bring the children. I see the children growing up, so I can tell. I can see the result. And also on my children, my sons – I can see it on them. Everywhere I go people say they are like little angels, although they are very different. It is because we were very strict [in following the tradition].

Jenny: So this is a long tradition, it has been around a long time…

Daliya: I guess from the beginning of time.

Colombia

Madame Josefa Morales De Garcia is an energetic, vivacious 75-year-old mother of seven, and a grandmother of 12. She has a small hotel in the city of Tunja, in the Colombian Andes, and is a dressmaker by occupation, now semi-retired.

Josefa was interviewed for me by her son, Orlando, at her

home in Tunja. The interview was later continued by Skype from New Zealand. This time I interviewed Josefa, Orlando, and Josefa's daughter, Maribel, translated. Traditionally Colombia has practiced 'the 40 days', la cuarentena, for many generations, although the practice has lessened in recent generations, especially in the cities. At the time of the interview, there was only one traditional midwife still practicing birthing and postnatal care in Tunja, and it was not possible to interview her. In spite of the decline, Colombian mothers still take very good care of their daughters in the weeks after childbirth.

Jenny: How were the births of your children?

Josefa: The births of my children were with what we call today a midwife, a traditional midwife who also directs the care of the mother after the birth. Apart from my first child, they were born at home and there was no need for hospitals. They were born naturally, with no complications.

For my first child I had a caesarean. This was because when I got married and got pregnant, I was only 14 years old, and I was still leading my normal teenage life, jumping and running around. I didn't care too much about slowing down, just running around everywhere, so my son got into a breech position - they found this out at the time of labour. So for this first one I went into hospital – but as soon as I got home the traditional midwife took over. For my next five children I took more care, and they were natural births. I went to hospital just after the sixth baby, but this was to have my tubes tied (a tubal ligation), then back home again to be cared for.

Jenny: How were you cared for after their births?

Josefa: I always had special care for the first 30 days, and then I had ten days of slowly coming back to my normal routines. I stayed for 30 days with no physical activity, and no going out. Generally I had very good care, especially from my own mother who had 16 children herself. The midwife came every day and my mother looked after me for 24 hours a day, bathing the baby and making sure I had everything.

Jenny: Didn't you find it hard to stay home and rest when you were so young with your first, and your friends were all out socializing?

Josefa: No, for the first one, I was so completely in love with my baby that I didn't want to do anything or go anywhere. I was completely into caring for the baby. For the other ones it wasn't quite so intense, but I stayed and rested all the same, and had the same level of care each time, until the last two. There was an eight-year gap between my first four and then my last two, and in that time a change was already starting to happen. The role of traditional midwives had started to become less important. My mother still cared for me 24 hours a day, but the midwife played less of a part. For the last two babies I didn't complete la cuarentena, I only did 25 days. But I still felt well.

Jenny: What about support from the rest of the family and the community?

Josefa: The whole family was very close to us during this period. My family supported me with company and help: my sisters, aunties and uncles, the extended family. A group of friends would come and bring food too, and help care for the baby, but my mother was always the main one looking after the baby. All the care and first baths of the baby would be done by her, not me. They bathe the baby very early on, not like the mother, every day from the first day. They used to add milk to the bath water because water by itself is too rough for baby's skin.

Jenny: What other special care did you receive?

Josefa: Traditionally, the mother and baby were kept in a darkened room for one week after the birth to protect the eyes. This was for the benefit of both the mother and baby, but it was kept more strictly for the baby. Actually it was important to be quiet and protect all of the senses from being over-stimulated, eyes, ears, everything. The baby has just come from the inside world of the mother into the outside world, and that transition needs to be slow and gentle. Since this tradition is not followed much now, I notice that children are less calm. Some people see this as a good thing, but I see it as a bad thing.

The mother doesn't have a bath after the birth, just a wash every day for 30 days. No full bath. The midwife and my sisters would wash me with a warm cloth. It is important to keep warm always, because you need to conserve energy after the birth. They would make sure I wasn't using my energy up keeping warm and I was always well covered. You need to be warm to keep a good blood supply moving too. The other traditional thing is that you shouldn't go out outside at the *sereno* [the twilight at dawn and dusk], when there is often a chilly wind. Your body can more easily catch cold at this time of the day; even if there is a cold wind later on in the day too, your body is most susceptible at the *sereno. [Note: From a Chinese medical perspective twilight is a transition time when yin (night) changes to yang (day) at dawn, and vice versa at dusk. During any transition, whether it is simply between day and night, during the menstrual period, or during the postpartum, there is greater potential for the qi to change rapidly, and therefore become destabilized more easily, than at other times. Therefore it made sense to give this advice to the postpartum woman who is already vulnerable because of the transition she is undergoing after childbirth.]*

Josefa's daughter Maribel: After 15 days, when the organs have had time to settle back in place, the mother is massaged and her hips wrapped. This is to tone the organs and help steady them in place as the mother heals. It protects the pelvic floor and keeps the lower abdomen warm also. For 40 days the midwife would come every day and check mum as well as the baby, massage her and bind her hips. So the mother was wrapped, and baby was also wrapped with a belt around the waist to make sure the umbilicus healed, and the tissues as well as the energy at the baby's navel was kept strong.

Jenny: How was your diet?

Josefa: They gave us chicken every day, and the broth of the chicken is thought to be even more valuable than the flesh. The tradition of having chicken broth was very important and we paid a lot of attention to it. It helps you to recover your strength and it helps the milk. There were no supermarkets then, and so you had to have your hens alive, ready in the yard, for the next 30 days. We also have poached eggs with a combination of herbs just after the birth: cumin, and especially *poleo*[6], followed by the chicken broth. Fruit intake was reduced for 30 days: they say that when you are losing blood you shouldn't have too much raw fruit, so this is true during your period as well. Also, the mother avoids greasy and deep-fried food. Nothing at all was eaten cold. After 21 days you started to drink a dark beer [like Guinness]. It was very nutritious and good for the breast milk, but this too was always given warm. *[Note: In general, keeping a balance of warming and cooling foods are a traditional Colombian way to maintain harmony in the body, and promote good health. Since after childbirth the mother is considered to be in a relatively 'cold' state, she restores the balance through eating warm and warming foods, while at the same time avoiding food which is cold, such as raw fruit. She also avoids food which is too 'hot', i.e. too spicy or stimulating, such as coffee and chilli. This theory goes beyond diet alone to the maintenance of a warm environment for the mother, covering herself well and avoiding the cold, as Josefa has mentioned earlier.In this respect, it is very similar to the other traditions encountered in this book.]*

Jenny: How did you feel at the end of 30 days?

Josefa: I felt absolutely fine, there were no complaints at all. Emotionally I felt really well, no depression. None of the women I knew then had psychological problems after childbirth. That is a disease of modern times.

Traditionally, the care of the mother is for 40 days with intensive care, support and company. That is why it is called la cuarentena. After 30 days, over ten days you are slowly integrated into normal life, so that by 40 days you are ready to go back into normal life. It was easy for me as dressmaker, because I worked at home, to slowly return to work while looking after my babies. Usually, I breastfed for a year.

Jenny: What is the role of men in la cuarentena?

Josefa: Everyone was involved in caring – my dad, husband and brothers. They were very caring and tried to help and be attentive as much as they could, asking always what they could do. But they were not the major support: their role was much less 'hands-on' than the role of the women around me. Nowadays the husband is more active in caring for the mother.

Jenny: Does the government help at all?

Josefa: The government gave no support, especially as we were independent - we didn't work for the government, so things were different.

Jenny: What was the most important thing for you after the birth? What sort of help?

Josefa: I didn't want to be by myself. I felt secure with people around me and having the special care of my mother. Also I appreciated the help of the midwife who helped me to breastfeed correctly and to produce good milk which was flowing well.

Jenny: Is the tradition of la cuarentena still followed today?

Josefa: One of my granddaughters has done la cuarentena, including the wrapping of the hips after 15 days. She rested totally for 40 days and reduced her weight slowly after the birth, not aggressively. But modern mums in the city generally don't follow the old tradition, partly because there are no longer many traditional midwives, so the traditional expertise is not there. Also families now have one or two children, whereas my mother had 16 children - the extended family is much smaller, with fewer women to help.

One part of the tradition which continues to be very important, though, is that the grandmother, the mother's mother, comes to look after her after she has given birth. I looked after my own daughters very carefully and gave them total care, and this is still done. The daughter calls up her mother on the phone and asks her to come and help, and she will come, a long way even, if she has to.

***

1. Shea butter is rich in vitamins A and E. It helps in tissue repair, relaxes the fine muscles on the skin surface and improves circulation. The effect is calming, refreshing and mildly warming.

2. Honey is known to improve beneficial gut bacteria and hence the immune system. For more information see A. C. Logan. *The Brain Diet* (Cumberland House, 2007).

3. Ghee, or clarified butter, is a food with special health-giving properties, in Ayurvedic (traditional Indian) medicine. It supports *ojas*, a bodily essence which is at the basis of vitality, enhancing tissue health and balancing hormones. It ensures a strong mind and body. Milk and almonds also support *ojas*. Ghee is especially good to build vitality as it improves the assimilation of nutrients, promotes the healing of injuries and reduces gastrointestinal inflammation. As it also calms the nervous system it is very helpful in healing after birth and in facilitating a smooth psychological adjustment to motherhood.

4. Women who give birth in Auckland City Hospital or another hospital with a normal vaginal birth are generally expected to transfer after three to five hours postpartum to Birthcare maternity hospital for three nights of free postnatal care.

5. Cited in K. du Fresne. 'Have We Got Immigration Right?', *New Zealand Listener*, 20 July 2013.

6. Poleo (*Hedeoma drummondii*) is a pungent, mint-like herb which is rich in antioxidants and is therefore useful in healing. It also has an antimicrobial function which protects against gastrointestinal infection.

Chapter Six

Meeting the Postnatal Challenge Today

The purpose of the Golden Month is for mothers to benefit from the care of family, community and the health system so they can recover after birth and re-enter society in good health. In order for this to happen, the postpartum needs to be recognized as a critically important time for women and their social, physical and emotional health. This has been emphasized throughout the book.

Authors Wertz and Wertz identify a paradox of modern medicine in favouring major interventions over providing basic preventive care.[1] In the modern developed world, basic preventive care after childbirth is not given sufficient attention. The mother often goes home from hospital after the birth to be alone with her partner, without community support. She feels lonely and tired and her morale goes down. As a result many women suffer from problems such as postnatal depression and exhaustion that significantly affect their well-being. In other societies where the community strongly supports six weeks of postnatal care, the opposite is true. She and the baby rest well and are looked after by older women while the younger brothers and sisters, partners and other family members do household chores and cooking.

Traditional practices are important during a major life change such as becoming a mother. On a social level they keep us 'grounded' in who we are, so that we can make a safe transition to motherhood. Different cultures also have different understandings of the human body through which they interpret the changes of the postpartum. Modern biomedicine is one way of understanding the body, and Chinese medicine, for example, is another way. The Chinese/Oriental medical view of the human body is at the basis of East Asian postnatal practices, and other traditional medicines inform their own postnatal practices. These views clearly have much in common when it comes to caring for new mothers, and when they are considered together they can reinforce and enrich our understanding of what happens in the postpartum.

It is also true that for traditions to remain meaningful and useful to the 'modern' woman, they must be flexible around changing lifestyles and changes in the family structure. It is common now to have grandparents who live far away, single mothers, cross-cultural marriages, nuclear families where the partner works long hours, and so on. This is where understanding the fundamentals and knowing what mothers need for their recovery can be resourcefully applied to suit the individual situation.

The 'stork story' is an example of how one group of mothers established a successful support system in their small community. It is a story of how traditional practices can evolve in modern situations:

> This is a tradition that six of us working mothers started. We all lived in the same street and we all got pregnant within a few months of each other. We started to meet together and decided on a plan to support one another after we had given birth.

In the Netherlands, where I am from, people put a wooden stork on the chimney to announce the birth of a baby, and my neighbour who was German had the same custom. So we made a stork out of plywood - he cut it out and I painted it. It was quite big, about 1.5 metres and it had a pole to tie it to the letterbox. It would appear on the letterbox when a new baby came, with a pink ribbon round its beak for a girl and a blue one for a boy. It was a signal that the new mother and her household would have a meal prepared for them by the others every night for two weeks after the birth.

So the six of us started doing this, and they weren't just any old meals that we produced either. These were real gourmet meals, cooked with love, and there was always so much food each time that it would last for two meals, so in the end there was enough for meals for one month. It was wonderful to receive a meal each night - just a simple thing, but very important.

Another thing I remember was those around me being able to take time, to slow the pace. Once while I was sleeping my midwife waited two hours for me to wake. She didn't want to disturb me. For me it was wonderful – a moment of absolute caring. It wasn't even an issue for her. She just talked to my mum for the time. Western culture is so much about being busy and doing things, so this was huge.

After a while the tradition grew from the original six to almost half of the 60 families in the street. We would cook for new families who came into the street too. Over time it strengthened us as a

> community and helped us to support each other in different ways: we enjoyed the relief of sharing our feelings as mothers at the end of the day, for example. As they got bigger the children spent a lot of time together and organized things like Halloween and camping. Some older people in the street even became surrogate aunties for those whose extended families were not around. Even though we let the tradition go when the children were older, valuing the importance of a supportive community has filtered down and stayed with them as young adults.
>
> It is not easy to get support for mothers after childbirth in modern city life. Our idea of cooking for each family for those first two to four weeks after a birth grew into a network of support that went way beyond the first month. It was a simple act, done with love, and it had a big impact. - *Tineke, New Zealand, originally from the Netherlands*

In Australia, New Zealand, the UK and USA, there are many informal groups and social networks where friends get together to prepare meals for the mother and help her with housework after the birth. The generosity and will to help other mothers is evident. In Westernized countries, however, the challenge of time means that this support is cut off after a couple of weeks.

The Netherlands has institutionalized postpartum care with the *Kraamverzorgster*, healthcare providers who visit the mother's home for a month after the birth to cook for her, do household tasks and care for her. There is also the system of the *doula*, increasingly popular in the USA, Western Europe and Australasia, who is a trained support person hired privately to care for mother and baby, to help her in childbirth and through recovery and the initiation into motherhood. In Korea and China, where it is now common to be living away from family support, postpartum hospitals and centres are available for some mothers to go for a month after birth. There has even been such a centre established for Chinese in New York. These hospitals provide the ingredients of a Golden Month: rest, a postpartum diet of warming, nutrient-rich food, massage, and a shared understanding with the mother of the importance of the month. Some Chinese mothers prefer to employ trained women who come into the house and perform the practices for the mother that her relatives would have done. *Zuo yue zi* ('doing the month') seems to be undergoing a revival in China where a high caesarean rate and the 'one child' policy have made women anxious to take the one opportunity they can after birth to recover properly and improve their health.[2] Many Asian couples living in the West also bring their parents out to live with them and care for mother and baby for several months after the birth. These are all ways of adapting to modern conditions, while keeping traditions alive. Although some may not include all of the essentials of good postnatal care, at the very least they allow the mother to rest and give her practical help.

Paid parental leave is also an important source of practical support for families after childbirth. At the same time it indicates how important family support is considered in different countries. Sweden, for example, has 16 months of paid parental leave at 80% of full salary (two of which must be taken by the father), and the countries of central Europe also offer extensive benefits. The UK has 39 weeks of paid leave, six of which are at 90% of full salary and the rest at a fixed rate. Most of the developing countries in Africa have 12–14 weeks at 100% of salary, despite the meagre resources of their health budgets. Australia has 18 weeks at a fixed rate (the minimum wage) and New Zealand 26 weeks. The US government, unfortunately, is the only one in the developed world to offer no paid leave.[3]

Beyond paid leave, however, it is important that our health-care systems actively support the fundamental principles of good postnatal care as an inherent part of encouraging a healthy family culture of the postpartum.

In their 2010 midwifery text, Sally Pairman et al. emphasize how valuable it is to have consistent messaging about postnatal care, and consider this as an important contribution to public health policy.[4] While changing our priorities within the family culture can inform public health practice, public health messages supporting the Golden Month can, in turn, change family culture.

The period after childbirth is an extraordinary transition in a woman's life which includes mother, baby and all those around her.

> The actual birth is not the end of the process. Afterwards, your body is open and vulnerable. They say in our culture that when you give birth, the 'tomb is open'. It is only after 40 days that the angels close the tomb. Please tell your women that they should rest for 40 days, stop work and look after themselves. – *Ngangouma*

When I re-read Ngangouma's words, I am reminded of how well she has encapsulated for me the reasons why we should encourage and support good postnatal practices and care for the mother as well as the newborn. As women, we recognize the qualities of courage, love and surrender it takes to go through childbirth. After each birth we are changed in a momentous way, on all levels, and it takes these same qualities to recognize our vulnerability, and allow ourselves to heal and enter motherhood. Following the practice of the Golden Month eases this process. From a practical standpoint, to do the best for ourselves does not mean following a rigid set of rules about how to eat and conduct ourselves after childbirth. Following our own Golden Month is essentially a question of understanding what is happening in the postpartum, recognizing the wisdom of our traditions and listening inward to the messages of our bodies – and then putting these three pieces of knowledge together, in the context of being held by family and community. This is how the essence of the Golden Month can be translated across cultures and ages.

Underlying everything is the status of the mother and the importance of motherhood. New mothers should be treated with the greatest care, for all the reasons that this book has outlined. After she has given birth, each mother is starting out on some of the most important work of her life and her baby's life. She deserves to be treated like a 'queen' as she nurtures her baby and herself through this rite of passage. We can all be part of changing our attitudes around the postpartum so that this can happen.

***

1. R.W. Wertz & D.C. Wertz. *Lying-in: A History of Childbirth in America* (Yale University Press, 1989), p.xiii.

2. N. F. Cheung, R. Mander, L. Cheng, et al. '"Zuo yue zi" After Caesarian in China: An Interview Survey', *International Journal of Nursing Studies,* 2006: 43(2): 193–202

3. ILO, 'Maternity and Paternity at Work: Law and Practice Across the World' Report International Labour Office, Geneva (2014), www.ilo.org/maternityprotection.

4. S. Pairman, S.Tracy, C. Thorogood and C. Pincombe, et al. *Midwifery: Preparation for Practice.* 2nd edn (Churchill Livingston, 2010), p.576.

Bibliography

Bawany, A. 'Steamed, Dehydrated or Raw: Placentas May Help Moms' Post-Partum Health; UNLV Anthropology Survey Examines Why Women Consume their Placenta After Childbirth', *UNLV Magazine*, Summer 2013, https://www.unlv.edu/news/article/steamed-dehydrated-or-raw-placentas-may-help-moms%E2%80%99-post-partum-health.

Buckley, S. J. Gentle Birth, Gentle Mothering: *A Doctor's Guide to Natural Childbirth and Gentle Early Parenting Choices* (Celestial Arts, 2009).

Byrom, S., Edwards, G. and Bick, D., eds. *Essential Midwifery Practice: Postnatal Care* (Wiley Blackwell, 2010).

Cartwright Jones, C. 'Traditional Postpartum Rituals of India, North Africa and the Middle East: Seclusion, Henna, & 40 day Homecare', *Born to Bloom: Resources for Women's Development, Aware Birth, and Beyond*, 2002, website: http://www.lotusfertility.com/Postpartum_Wisdom_Rituals.html.

Chatzi, L., Melaki, V., Sarri, K., et al. 'Dietary Patterns During Pregnancy and the Risk of Postpartum Depression: The Mother-Child 'Rhea' Cohort in Crete, Greece', *Public Health Nutrition*, 2011; 14(9): 1663–70.

Chatzi, L. Private correspondence with the author, 2014.

Cheung, N. F., Mander, R., Cheng, L., et al. '"Zuo yue zi" After Caesarian in China: An Interview Survey', *Int. Journal of Nursing Studies*, 2006; 43(2): 193–202.

Chu, C. M.Y. 'Postnatal Experience and Health Needs of Chinese Migrant Women in Brisbane, Australia', *Ethnicity and Health*, 2005; 10(1): 33–56.

Dennis, C. L., Fung, K., Grigoriadis, S., et al. 'Traditional Postpartum Practices and Rituals: A Qualitative Systemic Review', *Women's Health*, 2007; 3(4): 487–502.

Doidge, N. *The Brain that Changes Itself: Stories of Personal Triumph from the Frontiers of Brain Science* (Scribe, 2010).

Fava, M. and Mischoulon, D. 'Folate in Depression: Efficacy, Safety

Differences in Formulations and Clinical Issues', *Journal of Clinical Psychiatry*, 2009; 70(supp. 5): 12–17.

Fiengo, L., Bucci, F., Patrizi, G., et al. 'Postpartum Deep Vein Thrombosis and Pulmonary Embolism in Twin Pregnancy: Undertaking of Clinical Symptoms Leading to Massive Complications', *Thrombosis Journal*, 2013; 11(4), http://www.thrombosisjournal.com/content/11/1/4.

Gordon, M. *Roots of Empathy: Changing the World Child by Child* (Thomas Allen/The Experiment, 2009).

Grigoriades, S., Erlick Robinson, G., Fung, K., et al. 'Traditional Postpartum Practices and Rituals: Clinical Implications', *La revue Canadienne de Psychiatrie*, 2009; 54(12): 834–40.

Harkness, S. 'The Cultural Mediation of Postpartum Depression', *Medical Anthropology Quarterly*, June 1987; 1(2): 194–209.

Heh, S. S., Coombes, L. and Bartlett, H. 'The Association Between Depressive Symptoms and Social Support in Taiwanese During the Month', *International Journal of Nursing Studies*, July 2004; 41(5): 573–9.

Hibbeln, J. R. 'Seafood Consumption, the DHA Content of Mothers' Milk and Prevalence Rates of Postpartum Depression: A Cross-national Ecological Analysis', *Journal of Affective Disorders*, May 2002; 69(1–3): 15–29.

Huang Di Nei Jing [Yellow Emperor's Classic of Internal Medicine] Authors unknown. c. 500 BC.

Kokanović, R et al, (eds). Paths to Parenthood: Emotions on the Journey through Pregnancy, Childbirth, and Early Parenting (Palgrave Macmillan, 2018).

Krebs, N. F. 'Zinc Supplementation During Lactation', *American Journal of Clinical Nutrition*, August 1998; 68(2 supp.): 509s–512s.

Leahy-Warren, P., McCarthy, G. and Corcoran, P. 'Postnatal Depression in First-time Mothers; Prevalence and Relationships Between Functional and Structural Social Support at 6 and 12 Weeks Postpartum', *Archives of Psychiatric Nursing*, June 2011; 25(3): 174–184.

Lee, D. T. S. 'Postnatal Depression in Hong Kong Chinese'. PhD diss., Chinese University of Hong Kong, 2000.

Leung, B. M. and Kaplan, B. J. 'Perinatal Depression: Prevalence, Risks and the Nutritional Link - a Review of the Literature', *Journal of the American Dietary Association*, September 2009; 109(9): 1566–75.

Logan, A. C. *The Brain Diet: The Connection Between Nutrition, Mental Health and Intelligence* (Cumberland House, 2007).

Maxwell, D. 'The Clinical Utility of the Concept of Jing in Chinese Reproductive Medicine', *Journal of Chinese Medicine*, 2012; 98

Miller L. J., and LaRusso, E. M. 'Preventing Postpartum Depression', *Psychiatric Clinics of North America*, March 2011; 34(1): 53–65.

Naish, F. and Roberts, J. *The Natural Way to Better Birth and Bonding* (Doubleday, 2009).

Niska, K., Snyder, M. and Lia-Hoagberg, B. 'Family Ritual Facilitates Adaptation to Parenthood', *Public Health Nursing*, October 1998; 15(5): 329–37.

Northrup, C. 'Adrenal Exhaustion', *Christiane Northrup*, M.D., website: http://www.drnorthrup.com/adrenal-exhaustion/ [last accessed October 2015].

Pairman, S., Tracy, S., Thorogood, C. and Pincombe, J. *Midwifery: Preparation for Practice*, 2nd edn (Churchill Livingstone, 2010).

Palmer, S. *Hei oranga mo nga wahine hapu o Hauraki i roto i te whare ora.* PhD diss., University of Waikato, 2002.

Pichard, P. *Healing with Whole Foods: Asian Traditions and Modern Nutrition*, 3rd edn, (North Atlantic Books, 2002).

Piperata, B. A. 'Forty Days and Forty Nights: A Biocultural Perspective on Postpartum Practices in the Amazon', *Social Science & Medicine*, October 2008; 67(7): 1094–103.

Prentice A. M., Spaaij, C. J., Goldberg, G. R., et al. 'Energy Requirements of Pregnant and Lactating Women', *European Journal of Clinical Nutrition*, February 1996; 50(supp. 1): s82–s111.

Rice, P. L. *My Forty Days: A Cross-Cultural Resource Book for Health Care Professionals in Birthing Services* (The Vietnamese Antenatal/Postnatal Support Project, 1993).

Selander, J., Cantor, A., Young, S. M. and Benyshek, D. C. 'Human Maternal Placentophagy: A Survey of Self-Reported Motivation and Experiences

Associated with Placenta Consumption', *Ecology of Food and Nutrition*, 2013; 52(2): 93–115.

Stern, G. and Kruckman, L. 'Multi-Disciplinary Perspectives on Post-Partum Depression: An Anthropological Critique', *Social Science and Medicine*, 1983; 17(15):1027–41.

Szalavitz, M. and Perry, B. D. *Born for Love: Why Empathy is Essential - and Endangered* (William Morrow, 2010).

Teter, B. B., Sampugna, J. and Keeney, M. 'Milk Fat Depression in C57B1/6J Mice Consuming Partially Hydrogenated Fat', *Journal of Nutrition*, 1990; 120(8): 818–24.

Tinh Thong Nguyen. Private discussions with author, 2013.

Wickham, S. (ed.). *Midwifery: Best Practice*, vol.5 (Butterworth Heinemann Elsevier, 2008).

Wertz, R. W. and Wertz, D. C. *Lying-in: A History of Childbirth in America* (Yale University Press, 1989).

Wilkinson, R. and Pickett, K. *The Spirit Level: Why Equality is Better for Everyone* (Penguin, 2010).

Zhao, X. *Reflections of the Moon on Water: Traditional Chinese Medicine for Women* (Vintage Press, 2006).

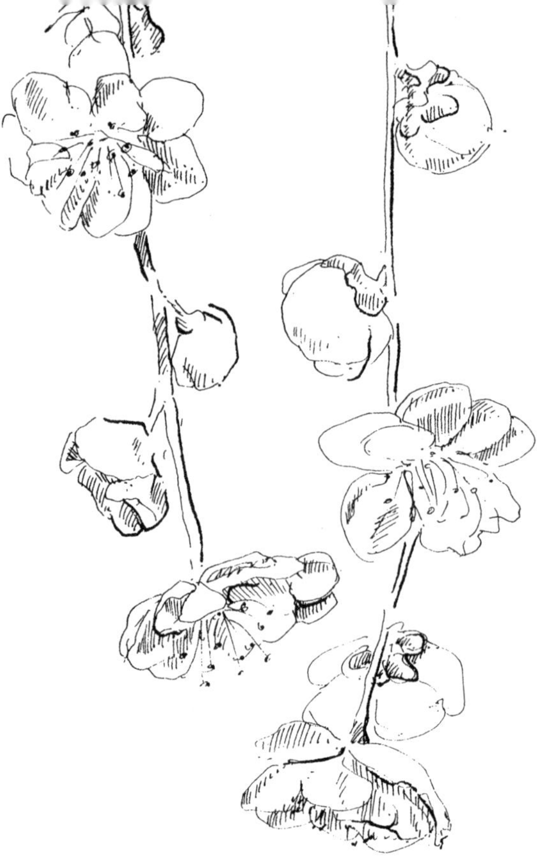